Contents

Page		Page	
2	Introduction to the Series	32	**Routes:** Teaching Notes
3	Ordnance Survey Mapping		**Routes Worksheets**
		33	1. School Journeys
		34	2. Local Journeys
6	**Viewpoint:** Teaching Notes	35	3. Choosing the best map
	Viewpoint Worksheets		
7	1. Playground furniture	36	**Grid References:** Teaching Notes
8	2. Table Top Jigsaw		**Grid Reference Worksheets**
9	3. Drawing Plans	37	1. The Invaders
10	4. Kitchen Plan	38	2. Rama and Sita
11	5. Classroom Plan	39	3. The Giraffe
12	6. Fairground	40	4. Ghosts and Ghouls
13	7. School Plan	41	5. Using 6 Figure Grid References
14	**Symbols:** Teaching Notes	42	**Location:** Teaching Notes
	Symbols Worksheets		**Location Worksheets**
15	1. Sorting sets	43	1. Classroom Locations
16	2. Matching Symbols and Pictures	44	2. Park Locations
17	3. Secret codes using symbols	45	3. Town Planner
18	4. Symbols in school	46	**Height:** Teaching Notes
19	5. Using O.S. Symbols		**Height Worksheets**
		47	1. Jelly on a Dish
20	**Direction:** Teaching Notes	48	2. Counting Contours
	Direction Worksheets	49	3. Interpreting Contours
21	1. Bully Goes Home (left and right)	50	**Using Photographs with Maps**
22	2. Safari Park	51	Aerial Photographs with Maps 1
23	3. Pet Shop	52	Aerial Photographs with Maps 2
24	4. In the Park		
25	5. Using Bearings		**Fieldwork Section**
		53	Fieldwork and Mapping
26	**Scale:** Teaching Notes	54	In and Around A Church
	Scale Worksheets	56	Exploring A Farm
27	1. The Castle	57	Urban Fieldwork
28	2. The Clown	58	Investigating A Castle
29	3. Kitchen Planner	59	Using Theme Maps and Old Maps
30	4. Bedroom Designer	60	**Answers to the Worksheets**
31	5. Recording to Scale	63	**Mapping Skills: Pupil Checklist**

Introduction to the series

The 'Discover and Master Maps with Ordnance Survey' series had its genesis in our feeling that much mapwork undertaken by pupils was divorced from the rest of the curriculum and from children's own experiences. Recent developments in schools have recognised the need to focus on the *application* of skills rather than the abstract acquisition of skills. We subscribe to the maxim that 'to do is to understand'.

The chief difficulty we encountered with much of the available 'mapping material' we had used with our pupils was a clear lack of opportunity for active participation, the use of imagination and a feeling of relevance. We therefore determined to look at the whole field from a fresh perspective.

Ordnance Survey were committed to the view that maps should offer more to pupils than merely a vehicle for answering a rather dull series of questions. The full resources of the OS were therefore made available to us and our selection of maps formed the core of the two pupil books.

The obvious dilemma for any authors of books which seek to provide the stimulating practice of map skills, is the degree of expertise which can reasonably be expected of pupils. The solution to the dilemma is the 'Ordnance Survey Resource File'. It is designed to support the teacher in a variety of ways.

Using the Resource File

Aspects of Mapping

Traditionally mapping has been subdivided into a number of aspects, each of which involves different but complementary concepts. In the Resource File we have broken down the Mapping development into eight key sections.

Viewpoint	Routes
Symbols	Grid References
Direction	Location
Scale	Height

There is a degree of arbitrariness about any such division but we have found it useful when working with mixed ability groups to use such an approach. It is systematic and it helps to pinpoint weaknesses which can then be remedied. Thus rather than saying — 'Gary can't read maps' — we would be able to say 'Gary can't understand contours'.

Each key section begins with a page of text. The page serves a number of purposes. It identifies the basic concept which the section develops. There are suggestions which refer to practical activities which might enhance pupil understanding and skill. This is followed by an analysis of each of the worksheets in the section. The teacher is then better able to identify the purpose of the worksheet, whether it is intended as an introduction, an extension or a reinforcement of a skill.

In each key section the worksheets offer consistency, continuity and progression. It is important however for teachers to use their professional judgement. The whole package is designed for a wide ability range and pupils who are already skilled and confident should not find themselves ploughing through exercises they could do standing on their heads.

It is also necessary to exercise judgement in the pace at which progress is made. It would be unsound to complete all the Viewpoint sheets before beginning the first Direction sheet. Skills developed in the early stages of one key aspect will be assumed in the later stages of another aspect.

To help teachers choose appropriate worksheets a chart is provided on each introductory page. It lists 'targets' for pupils under the headings of — 'to know' and 'to be able to do'. These targets are expressed in four stages of development. Thus teachers may begin by identifying the stage of development individual pupils have reached and deciding future strategy from there. It must be stressed that this is not an exact science, professional judgement and re-appraisal need to be used constantly. The targets do provide a broad framework which should prove helpful.

A second chart appears on each introductory page. It lists the key skills involved in each worksheet and it identifies the main points in the pupil textbooks where those skills are practised.

The main element of each key aspect is the series of worksheets. All worksheets are photocopy-free. We suggest an initial stock be copied but that pupil performance needs to be considered before larger runs of copying take place.

It will come as a great relief to many that answers to the worksheets are to be found on pages 60–62.

There is also a 'Pupil Checklist' on page 63. This is an individual pupil record which can be passed up the school with the child and will help to ensure curriculum continuity.

Fieldwork

The final section of the Resource File includes a series of suggestions for fieldwork activities. The Pupil textbooks use maps at locations such as farms, castles, churches etc. The teacher's notes are intended to provide ideas for visits to such sites, the emphasis is on using maps in such contexts but there are other suggestions relating to the wider potential of such visits.

PATRICIA HARRISON
STEVE HARRISON 1989

OS MAPS CAN IMPROVE THE QUALITY OF FIELDWORK

The Ordnance Survey — Historical Background

OS MAPS, PRODUCED TO HELP DEFEAT THE FRENCH

Pupils may wish to know about the history and work of the OS.

As the word 'ordnance' suggests the origins are military. The fear of an invasion from France caused the military to require accurate maps of the South Coast of Britain.

The 'Board of Ordnance', which at the time was responsible for artillery, armaments and army engineers, was given the task of surveying the land. The Ordnance Survey was founded in 1791. The first OS maps were drawn at a scale of 1" to 1 mile.

Demand for maps grew as others recognised their potential value. The survey was extended to cover the whole country and larger scales were introduced to provide more detailed information.

It is important to advise pupils that mapping did not begin with the OS in 1791. In 'Master Maps' we feature a map drawn in 1577 and many local libraries and museums stock reprints of early maps for their areas. It is useful to obtain a range of such maps for a variety of purposes (see below).

Choice of Maps

There is an enormous range of maps available and it is desirable that pupils are introduced to as wide a selection as possible. Wherever feasible this introduction ought to be in the context of an informed judgement on the selection of a specific map for a specific purpose. Children can then relate to the map as a resource relevant to the task in hand. The pedagogic function is to draw attention to the qualities/data a particular map offers when compared to other maps. Ultimately the ability to choose the best map is a skill we hope all children will acquire. All the abstract mapping skills in the world will not help you find the quickest route to your nearest Post Office if you have selected The Daily Telegraph Map of the World (Political) as your resource!

1:1250

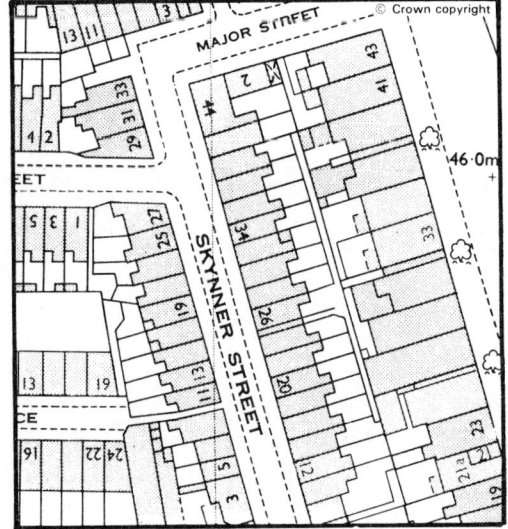

Range of Maps (OS)

LARGE SCALE:

Good practice starts from the child and the child's environment. Pupils will see the value and potential uses of maps if they see a local feature with which they are personally familiar represented in an accessible form. This could be the home, street, school, church, mosque, park etc. The important point is that it should be *their* school, park or street, known to them both by name, sight and experience.

There are three OS Large Scale Maps from which to choose.

1:1250 (1cm: 12.5m)
(50 inches: 1 mile)
This is the largest scale of map published by the OS. *It is available only for urban areas.*

This scale of map is ideal for younger children and for detailed work with older pupils.

The 1:1250 provides house numbers or names where appropriate. Pavements appear clearly and the detail is such that local work on street furniture or detailed measurement and survey activity can be successfully carried out using this scale.

1:2500 (1cm:25m)
(25 inches:1 mile)

This scale of mapping covers most of the country apart from sparsely populated areas of mountain and moorland. Large urban areas covered by the 1:1250 are not available in the 1:2500.

Detail is similar to the 1:1250 although obviously the size of individual features is halved and is therefore less attractive for detailed investigation work in the street. For most pupils however this is a very accessible scale of map and it sometimes has the advantage of providing pupils with both the specific feature they want to investigate (e.g. the school) and its immediate context (e.g. the catchment). In effect there is no choice between the two maps for the study of a specific location as they are mutually exclusive in the areas they cover.

- The 1:1250 maps cover an area 500m × 500m and the sheets measure 495mm × 572mm.
- The 1:2500 maps are mainly 2km East to West by 1km North to South although some are 1km × 1km.
- The 1km × 1km sheets are the same size as the 1:1250 (495mm × 572mm). The 2km × 1km are larger (899mm × 584mm). This has implications for storage and for pupil use. A large flat surface is needed and pupils will inevitably lean on the edges if they are to examine the centre of the map. It is a sensible strategy to cover the maps in a clear fabric.

1:10,000 (1cm:100m)

This scale of mapping is the largest available for the whole country. Mountains and moorland are shown and the maps are the largest scale using *contour lines*. Some areas are not yet available in the 1:10,000 format and can only be obtained in the old 6 inches to 1 mile scale (1:10560).

The 1:10,000 maps are mostly printed on paper 679mm × 559mm and cover an area 5km × 5km. They are invaluable for a range of relevant activities. They cover an area large enough to account for the bulk of many school's catchments. Pupil networks can therefore be plotted on them.

Individual rows of houses are shown. Thus local pupil surveys can add missing information e.g. door numbers, outbuildings etc.

The pattern of housing/recreation/shopping areas is much easier to see on a 1:10,000 than on any other scale. This is particularly useful if you want to look for street patterns and match them to dates of development. The centres of old established towns often reveal no clear pattern, but a hotch potch layout which evolved without planning. This compares with the geometry of Georgian housing and the uniformity of much Victorian working-class housing. The grid-plan industrial pattern can be compared in turn with modern housing estates complete with link roads, crescents and cul-de-sacs.

The 1:10,000 series is ideal for plotting traffic flow. A traffic census carried out at key points will generate data about flow and potential hazards. Pupils can tackle questions about one-way systems, bus lanes, locations of pelicans etc. Clearly such activities are also possible on the 1:1250/1:2500 maps but they would be on a much smaller focus and be specific. The 1:10,000 allows a wider approach and an opportunity to look at patterns and causal factors more easily.

A limited number of 1:10,000 maps are available in the 'town and city' series. These are particularly attractive to schools wishing to follow up activity investigation work. Leisure provision, transport and an index to road names all offer opportunities for development.

LARGE SCALE: OLD MAPS

As new surveys are completed, maps become obsolete. Many of such older maps are still held by the OS and schools can be supplied with copies. This is particularly useful for charting minor changes in an area. The change of use of a building or some limited clearance in an urban renewal programme are obvious examples. This helps pupils to understand the process of changes in the locality more easily than comparisons with a seventeenth century map where little that they can relate to remains. It is also worth considering making your school's own local detailed survey using an OS map of some years ago before comparing your results with the latest OS map.

1:25,000 (4cm:1km)
(2½in:1 mile) Covers an area 20km East to West × 10km North to South.

This series, known commercially as the *Pathfinder Maps* is easily recognised by its green cover (folded). Virtually the whole of the country is covered by this series. However, at the time of writing (1988) those areas not covered by the green series still have the blue 1st series edition available covering areas 10km × 10km. The series includes public rights of way.

It is an excellent scale to move to from the 1:10,000 in order to look at your own area in relation to other settlements. The streets, their housing configurations and even gardens can still be seen. 1:25,000 is the smallest scale of map where this is possible — such detail is not available on the 1:50,000. This series therefore provides a continuing personal link for the pupils between their school/homes and the wider setting.

Distances between settlements/centres can now be considered. Shopping/recreation/work routes can emerge. Public transport systems can be examined and comparisons can be made between communities based on

1:2500

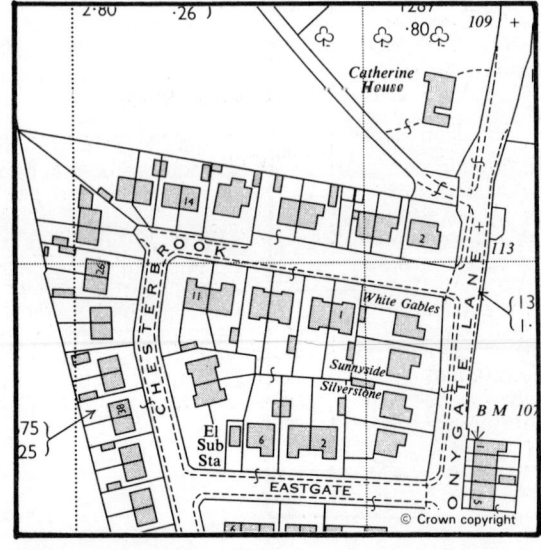

1:10 000

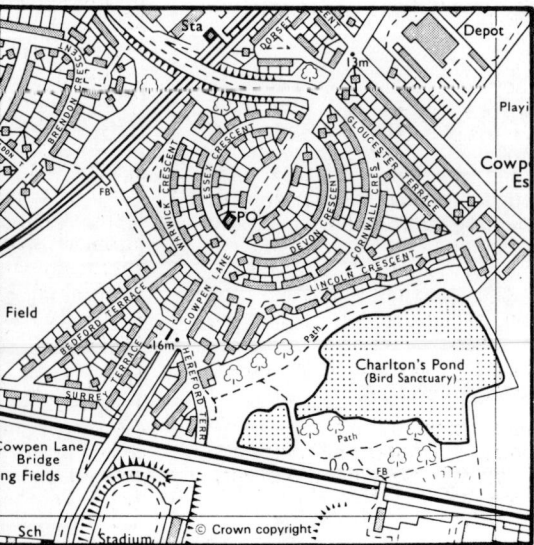

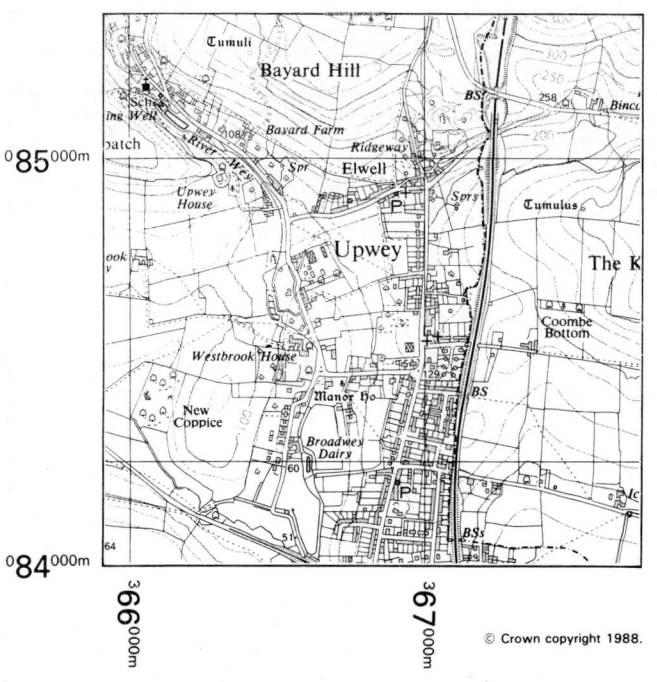

1:25 000

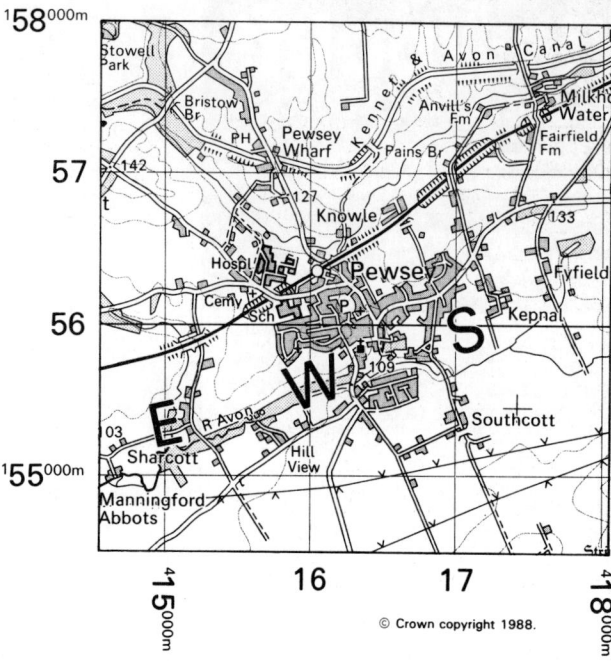

1:50 000

their location relative to amenities/major physical features/communications networks.

Walking an area is an essential aspect of using maps with a purpose and appreciating the potential that a map can offer. The 1:25,000 is useful for such activity. The rights of way are clearly marked and the series also has the great virtue of mapping the field system. Urban pupils can plan and execute a rural walk and often find the landmarks of field boundaries and isolated buildings/springs/small woods particularly useful in confirming they are on the right track. (Needless to say we assume the teacher will be offering advice and guidance at the planning stage, will walk the route in advance if not already known and that the pupil/teacher ratio will be in accordance with local advice.)

The colour key and ease of storage are other factors which make this series particularly attractive to schools.

1:50,000 (2cm:1km)
(1¼ in:1 mile)

This series is sold as the *Landranger Maps*. Each map covers an area 40km × 40km. It is less immediate for many children and is perhaps most useful with older pupils.

The 1:50,000 provides a great deal of information and pupils will need to focus in on what they want rather than risk confusion from too much data. We would suggest it is best used in considering aspects of your region: the major conurbations, the road and rail networks, place name analysis and tourist features.

In large conurbations the picture of a major centre with routes emerging from it to the satellite towns around is very easy to see.

The patterns of motorways, trunk roads and minor roads can also be examined and in so doing useful work undertaken in using and understanding a key.

This series is very useful if pupils are away on fieldwork which includes an element of travel by minibus or coach. The 1:50,000 series can be used in the vehicle for pupils to predict what is around the next corner — 'We will pass under a railway bridge/to the North will be a steep cliff/a wood to the South/the road winds for the next 2km etc.' We have found this of enormous value in helping pupils develop the language of maps, the use of keys, the capacity to relate the three dimensional world out there to the two dimensional representation in front of them — and as a bonus it reduces the incidence of travel sickness at a stroke!

Specific-Theme OS Maps

A number of historical maps are available from the OS. They provide a mapping perspective for the distribution of sites of specified periods (e.g. Roman Britain, Britain in the Iron Age). These have limited use for active participation but they are a very useful resource to go alongside a classroom theme. Essentially such a map demonstrates that whatever the centre of interest it is often possible to express an aspect of it spatially and that such an expression will
a) often demonstrate a pattern
b) that pattern may have a logical explanation which can be deduced.

There is a great deal of potential in the Victorian OS 1" series. This is a reprint of the survey published from 1805-1873. Direct comparisons with the children's present environment are made feasible by the use of this series.

Other Maps

Clearly the principal source of maps for pupils will be the OS. There are times when other sources will be appropriate and teachers need to be alert to such opportunities.

Foreign Maps

There is much to be said for using foreign maps in the classroom. The Michelin 1cm:2km series for France is available in many retail outlets in the U.K. and is a good size to handle. If the teacher asks a number of questions which require the use of the map (e.g. which roads would you follow to go from Fecamp to Le Havre?) pupils will soon realise that maps are written in an international language which can be decoded by anyone who understands maps in their own country. There are obviously limitations to the extent pupils can interpret the maps but many teachers are surprised by the degree to which pupils can transfer their skills to foreign maps.

U.K./World Maps

It is important to provide children with a view of maps which is not confined to their immediate locality or region. World or national maps can be displayed around the school. Items on the news, whether terrorism, natural disaster or royal visit can be referred to in the context of a reference to the map. A collection of letters can be related to locations in Britain, categorised by County. Family connections can be linked both to County maps and a World map.

Viewpoint

BASIC IDEAS

Understand the difference between side, oblique and plan views.
Understand the reason and need for maps.

	TARGETS FOR CHILDREN	
	TO KNOW	BE ABLE TO DO
STAGE 1	To know that the term 'plan' means view from above. Know the difference between picture/plan views. Know the difference between oblique and side views.	Draw simple plans of everyday objects. Match pictures and plans. Draw plan of table top. Draw basic plan of classroom. Compare oblique and plan views of objects.
STAGE 2	Know and recognise oblique and plan views of rooms. Know that plan means map. Know the relationship between aerial photograph and plan.	Able to draw a plan of a classroom reasonably accurately. Use a plan of school to locate points.
STAGE 3	Know and use terms plan, map, oblique, aerial, reduce, enlarge. Know that moving objects are not normally depicted on maps.	Draw a plan of classroom to scale. Locate points on plan of school using symbols and key. Use aerial photographs alongside local maps.
STAGE 4	Know that plan is normally a view from above. A plan is a 2 dimensional representation of a 3 dimensional object.	Draw plans to scale with little assistance. Make accurate comparisons between plan/aerial photo/ 1:25,000/1:50,000.

Children do not acquire mapping skills incidentally, they need to be taught in a structured way. Many eleven year olds with little exposure to maps draw their route to school and make basic errors. Houses are drawn flat, invariably detached, belching smoke and surrounded by a garden. The route will often show vehicles and people. This is similar in many ways to the work a six year old will produce, the amount of detail will differ but the basic failure to conceive of a map as a view from above is the same.

Starting Points

Fundamental to the concept of 'plan' is the idea that objects (including buildings) look different depending on how and from where they are viewed. The starting point is the same irrespective of age. All children need a large amount of practical observation and recording. They need to look, discuss and draw what they see from a variety of vantage points. It is best to begin with everyday objects — kettles, jugs etc. which when viewed from different directions and angles look different.

Children should be encouraged to look at the same object from two side positions and to discuss the differences in what they see. When they record their observations they should draw *only* what they can see, not what they know to be there (e.g. a handle).

Notes on Worksheets

Viewpoint 1 gives practice in viewpoints. Extension activities should provide opportunities to draw pictures and plans of ordinary artefacts found in the classroom.

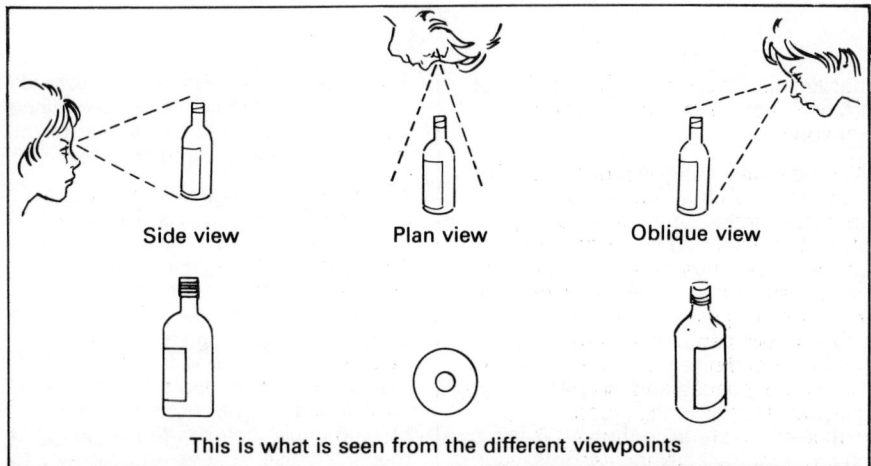

This is what is seen from the different viewpoints

At this stage it is sensible to define plan as 'a view from above'.

Once side view and plan view are known and understood oblique view should be added. The word oblique ought to be used as it is part of the vocabulary of mapping.

Viewpoint 1 matches a mixture of side and oblique views to plan views.
Viewpoint 2 focusses on oblique to plan. At this stage observation and recognition are required but the pupils are not expected to draw their own plans. **Viewpoint 3** adds the dimension of the child's own drawing. **Viewpoint 4** adds colour key in matching picture to plan. **Viewpoint 5** combines both elements of 3 and 4. The children must draw their own plan, devise a colour key and use it appropriately. It is important that by this stage they are aware not to draw people on a plan.

By now children should have a sound grasp of plan. The variety of shapes at the fairground will stretch the pupils and indicate the degree to which plan view is understood.

Viewpoint 7 uses a school plan, a plan of their own school should also be used for consolidation.

The skills developed in this section are used throughout the pupil textbooks.

WORKSHEET	SKILLS INVOLVED	SKILLS PRACTISED IN	
		BOOK 1	BOOK 2
1 Playground	Match picture/plan	p. 2/3 p. 6/7	p. 21
2 Tabletop Jigsaw	Matching oblique and plan views	p. 2	p. 8
3 Drawing Plans	Drawing plan from oblique view	p. 2	
4 Kitchen Plan	Comparing oblique and plan views	p. 28/29	
5 Classroom Plan	Interpret view and translate into plan	p. 2	p. 16/17
6 Fairground	Drawing plans of unusual shapes	p. 24	p. 7
7 School Plan	Interpreting a plan of a building	p. 2	p. 12

Viewpoint 1   Playground Furniture

Match the picture with the plan.

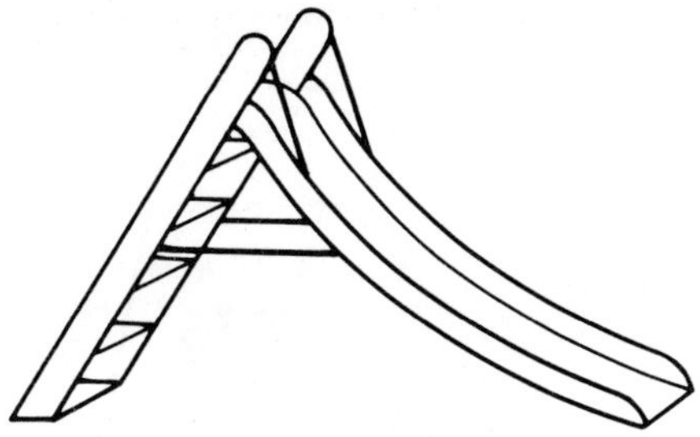

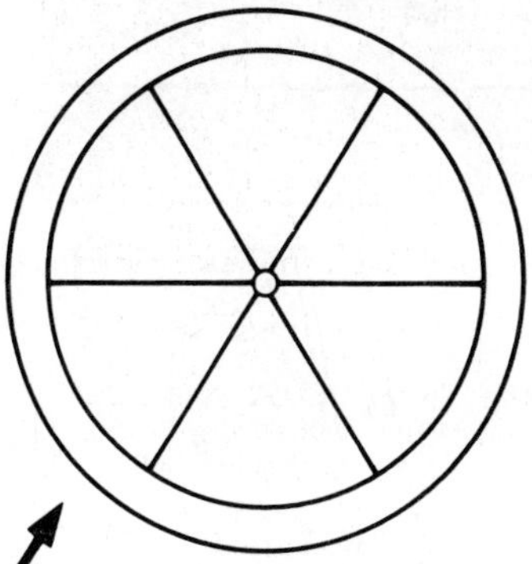

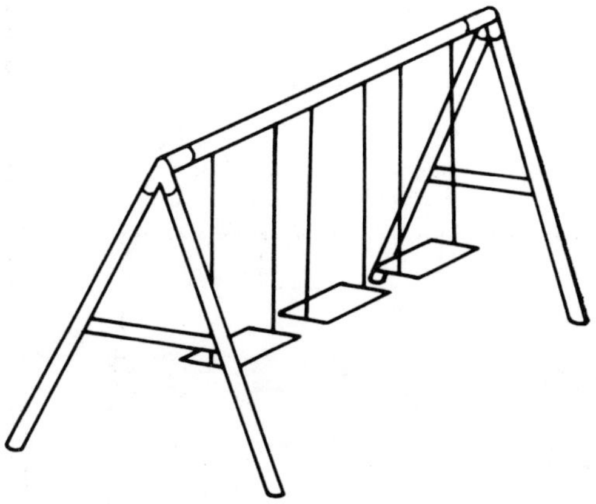

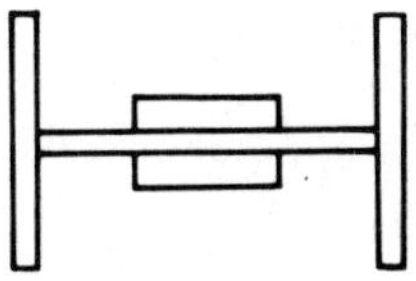

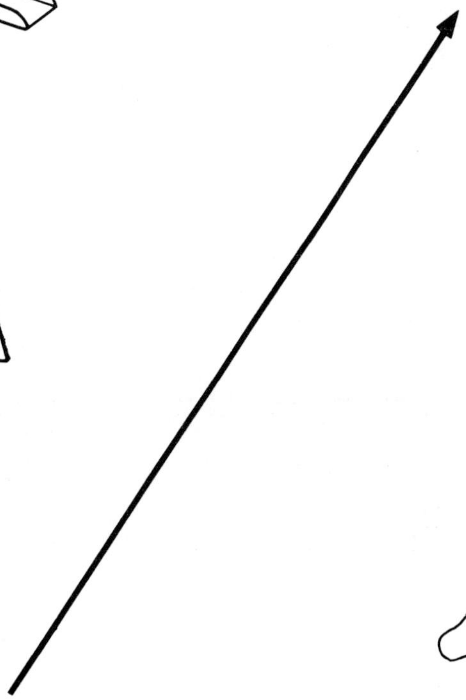

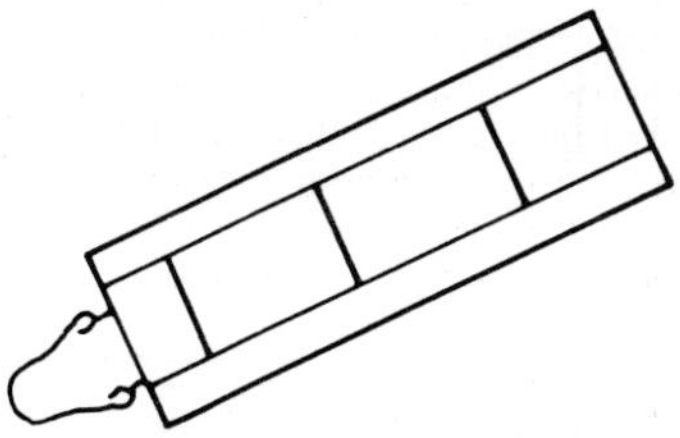

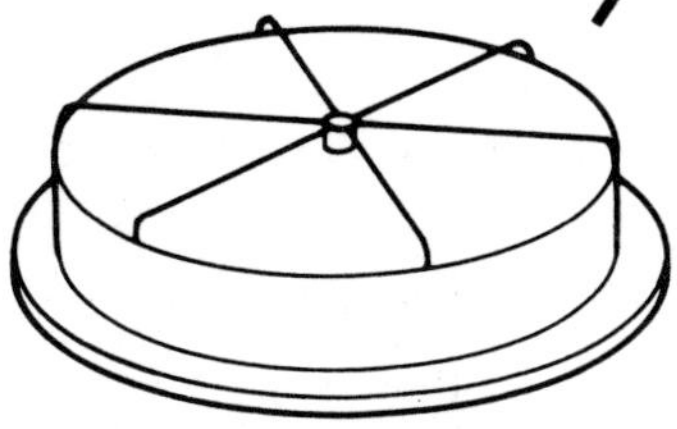

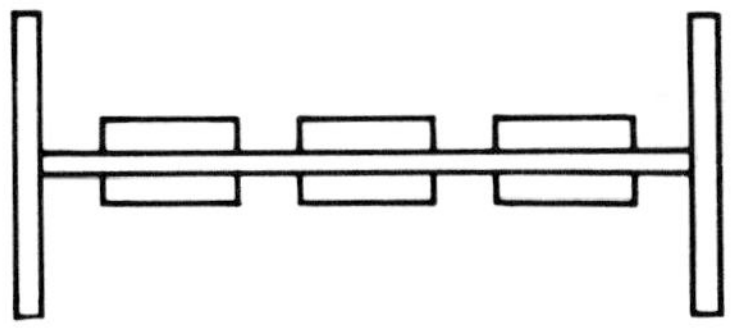

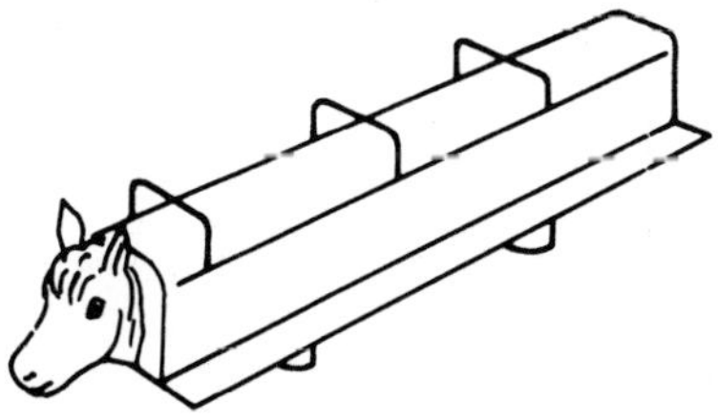

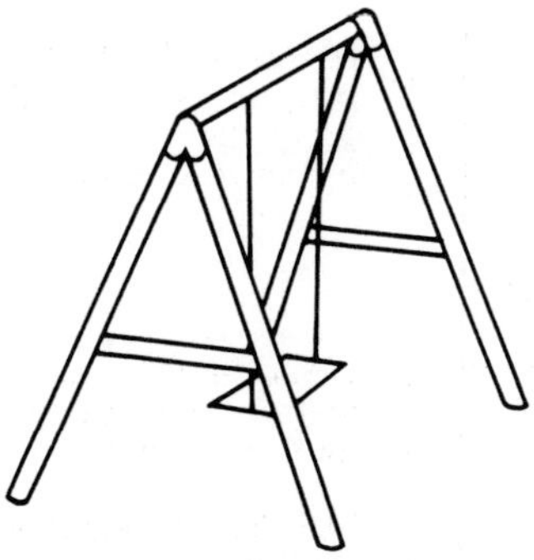

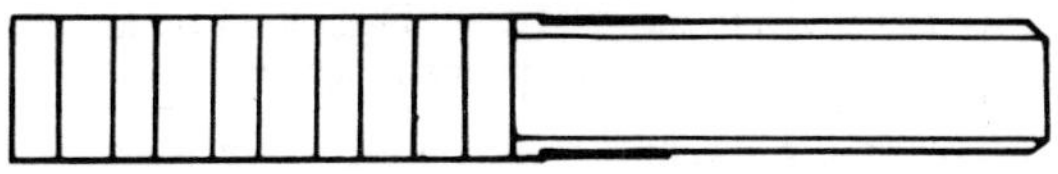

7

Viewpoint 2   Tabletop Jigsaw

Oblique view

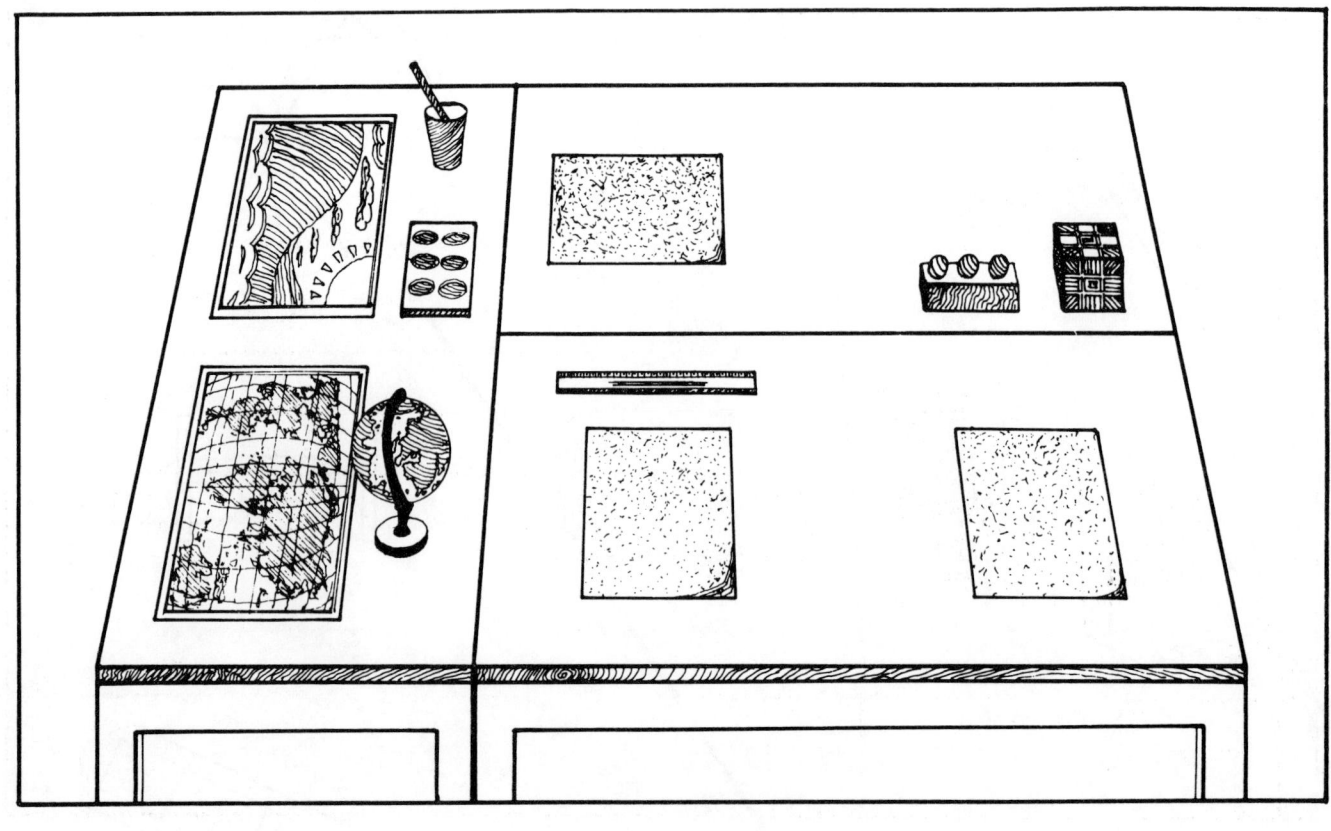

Plan view

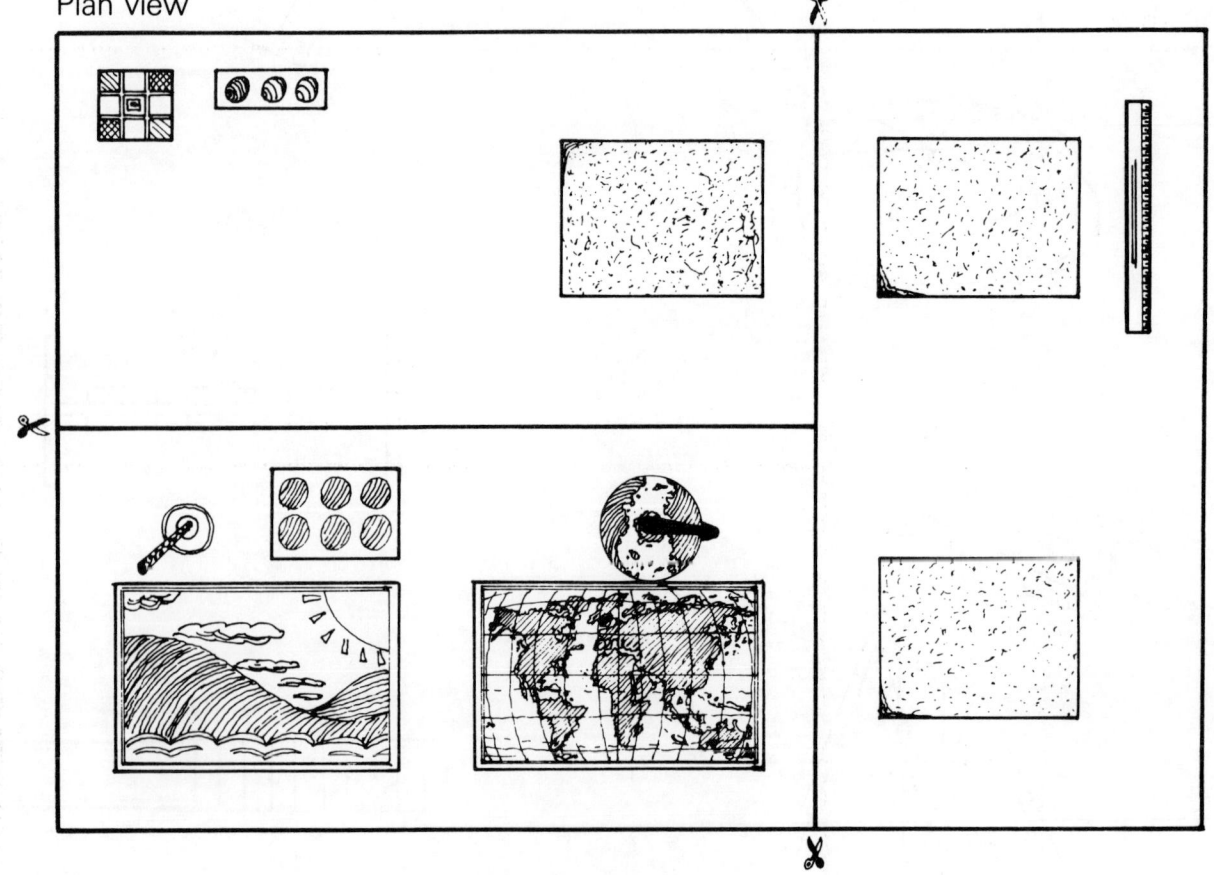

The plan view does *not* match the oblique view.
Cut out the tables and rearrange them to match.

Viewpoint 3   Drawing plans

Oblique view

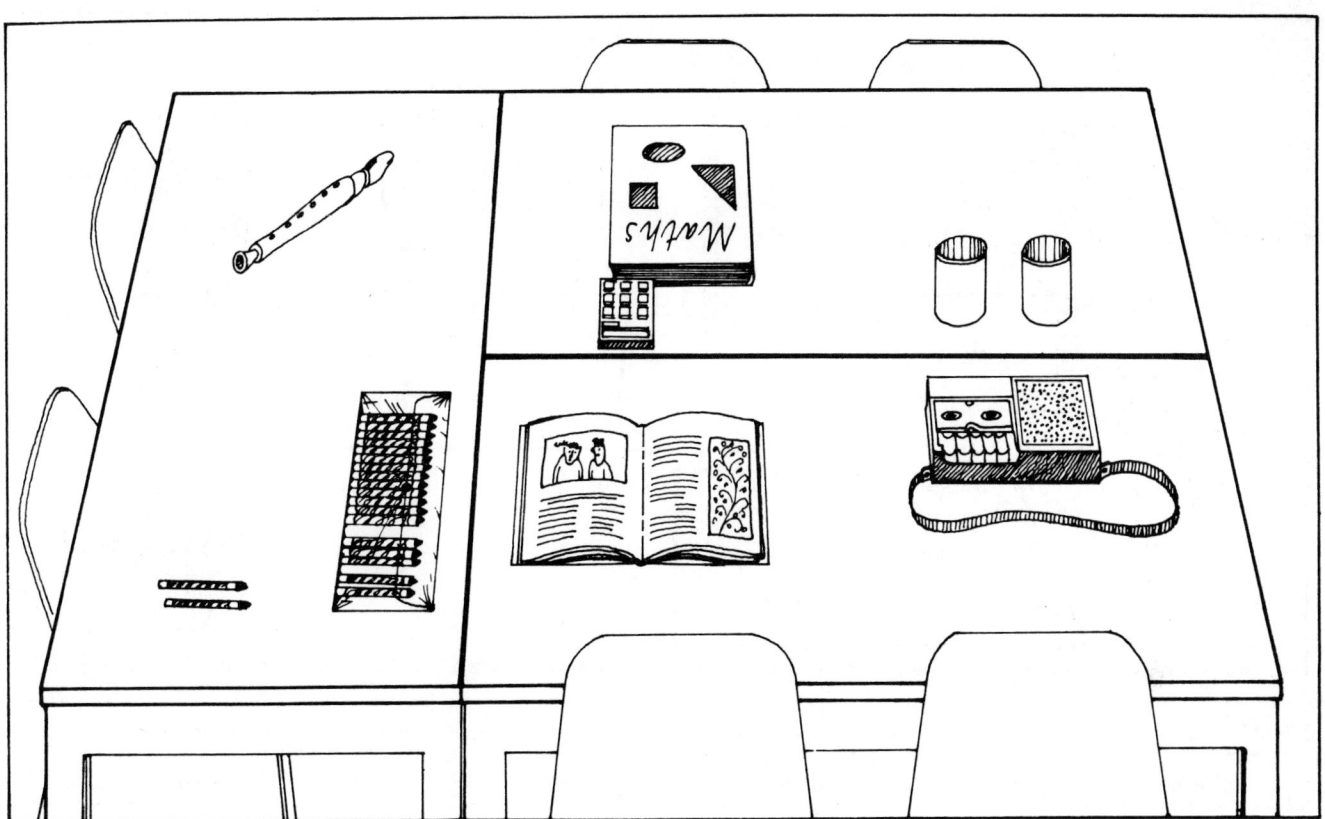

Plan view

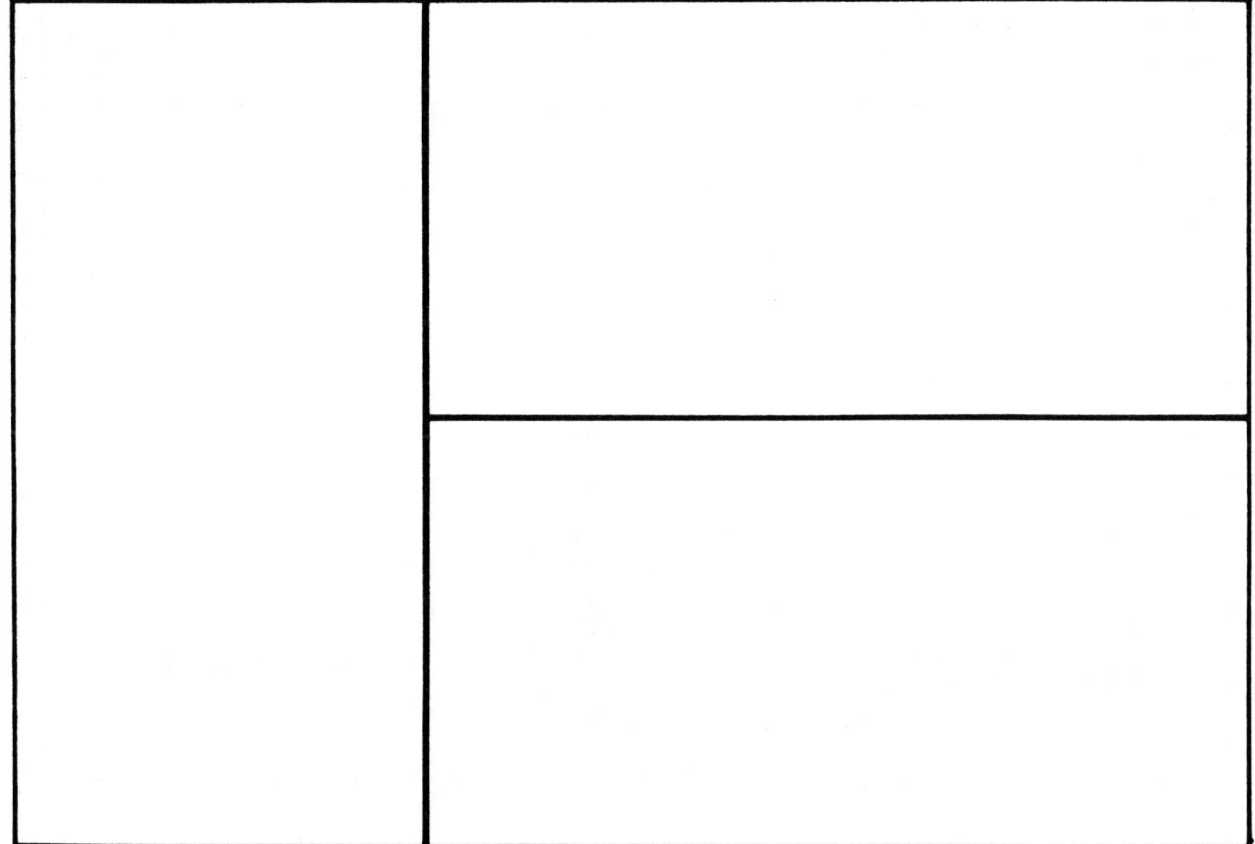

On the plan of the table draw the plan view of each object.
Draw a plan of your table or desk.

© Collins Educational: Harrisons/OS Resource Book ▶ You may photocopy this page for use in the classroom ◀

Viewpoint 4   Kitchen plan

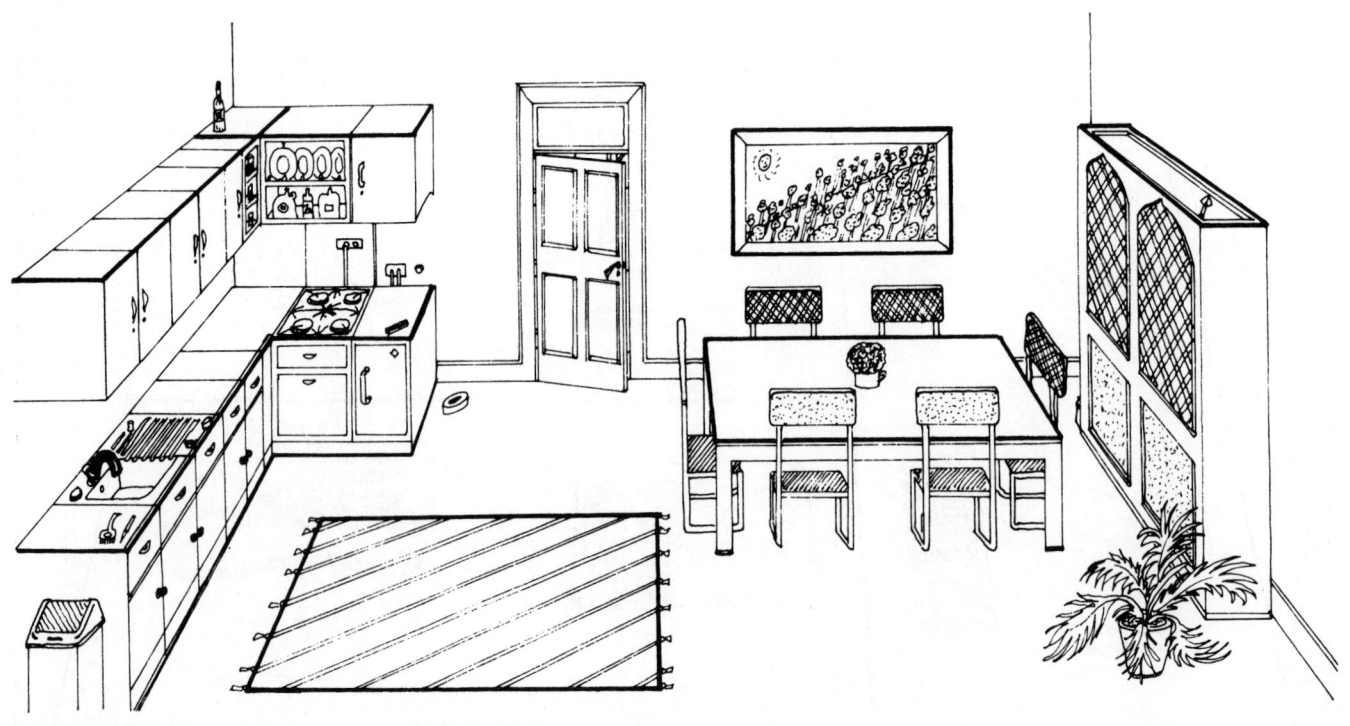

KEY					
black	Table	blue	Cooker	pink	Sink
red	Chairs	orange	Rug	yellow	Fridge
brown	Wall units	green	Plant	purple	Dining cabinet

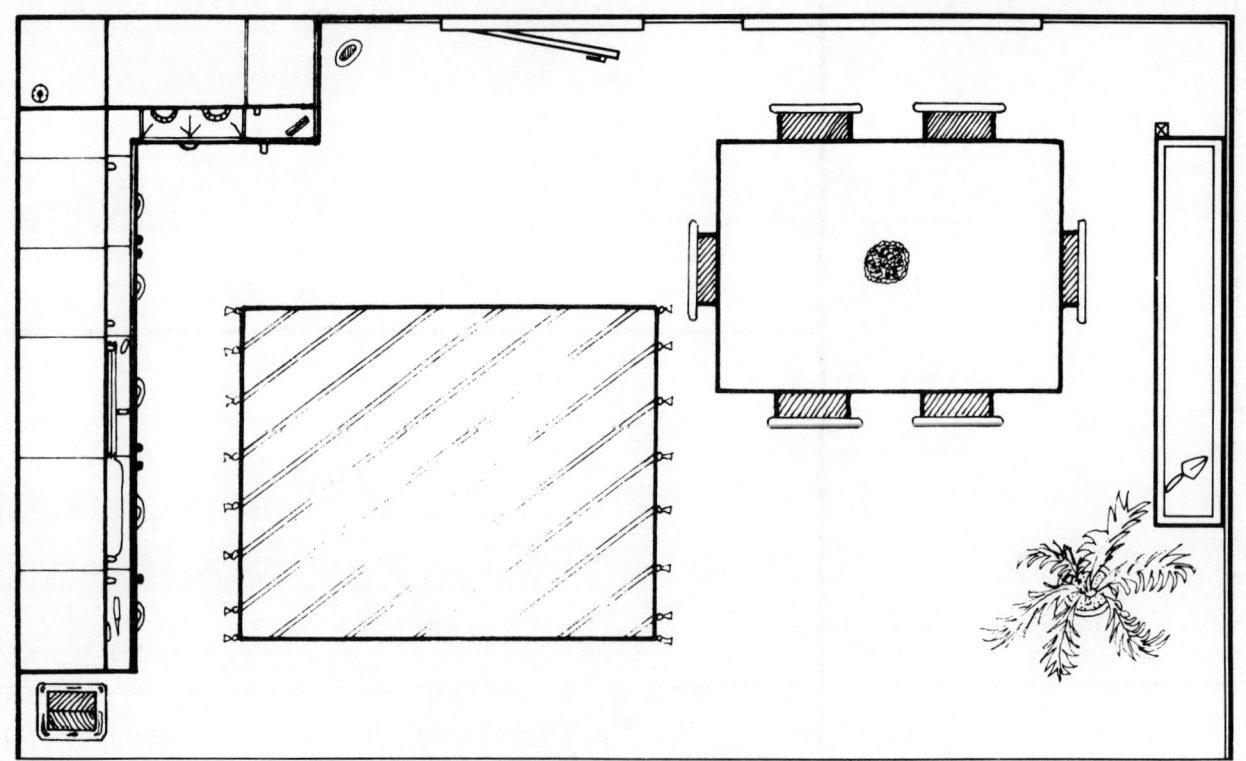

Look at the key.
Colour in the picture and the plan.

© Collins Educational: Harrisons/OS Resource Book ▶ You may photocopy this page for use in the classroom ◀

Viewpoint 5   Classroom plan

1 Draw on the plan view:

Door	Bookshelves
Windows	Maths table
Pupils' tables	Pupils' trays

2 Make a colour key.

| KEY | | Windows | | Pupils' tables | | Bookshelves |
| | | Door | | Maths table | | Pupils' trays |

© Collins Educational: Harrisons/OS Resource Book ▶ You may photocopy this page for use in the classroom ◀

Viewpoint 6   Fairground

Draw the plan view of the fairground.

Viewpoint 7   School plan

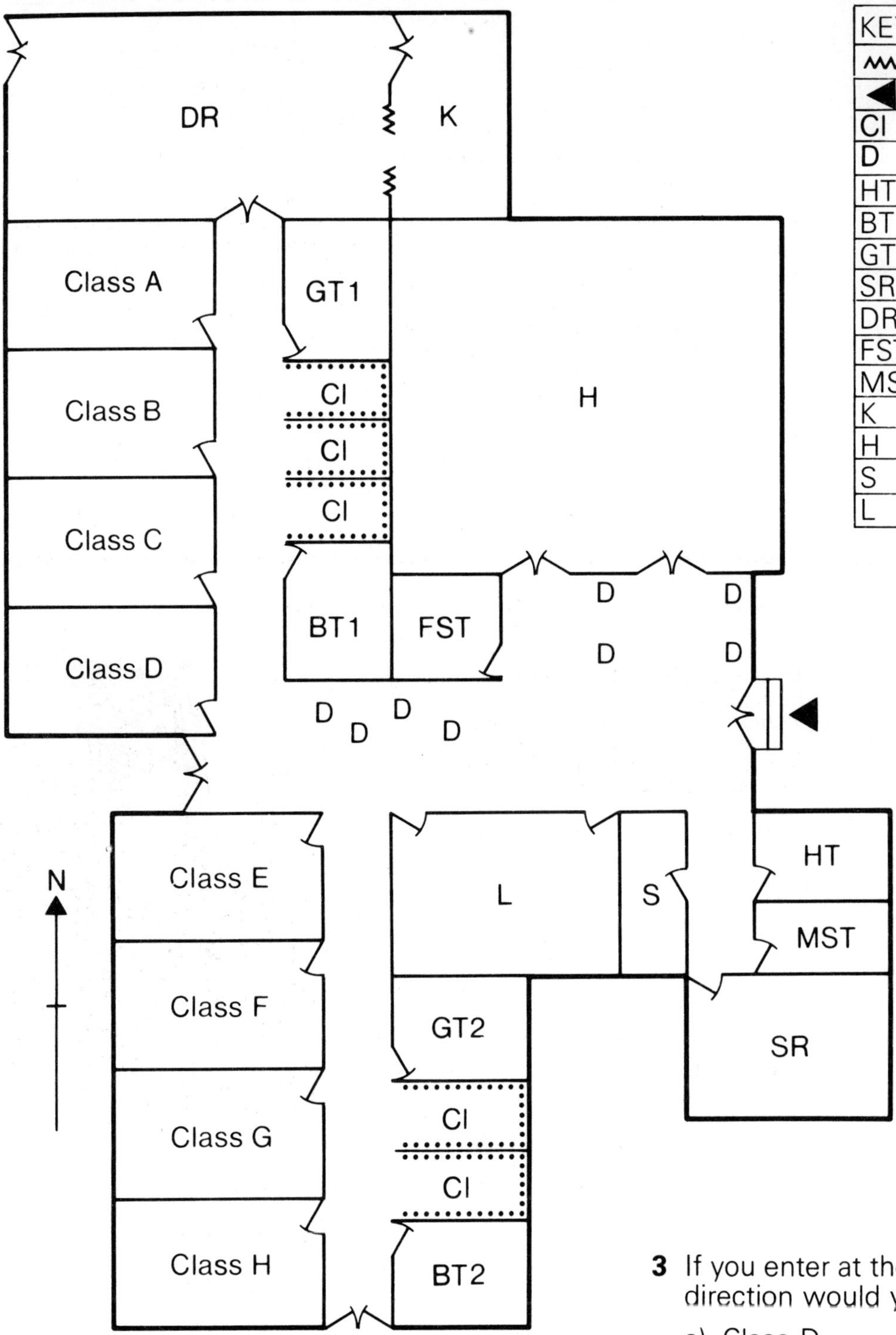

KEY	
ᴡᴡᴡ	Serving hatch
◀	Main entrance
Cl	Cloakroom
D	Display
HT	Headteacher
BT	Boys toilet
GT	Girls toilet
SR	Staff room
DR	Dining room
FST	Female staff toilet
MST	Male staff toilet
K	Kitchen
H	Hall
S	Secretary
L	Library

Task

1 Which room is **South** of

a) The headteacher's office   _____

b) The library   _____

c) The hall   _____

2 Which room is **North** of

a) Class A   _____

b) The staff room   _____

c) Girls toilet 2   _____

3 If you enter at the main entrance in which direction would you walk to reach

a) Class D   _____

b) The hall   _____

c) Staff room   _____

Use N.S.E.W.

4 On which side of the school is

a) The dining room   _____

b) Headteacher's room   _____

c) Class B   _____

d) Boys toilet 2   _____

5 Use a plan of your school. Make a key.

© Collins Educational: Harrisons/OS Resource Book ▶ You may photocopy this page for use in the classroom ◀

Symbols

BASIC IDEA

Understand why symbols are used and the need for a key.

	TARGETS FOR CHILDREN	
	TO KNOW	BE ABLE TO DO
STAGE 1	Know that symbols represent features. Know what a key is.	Make own symbols. Recognise a limited number of OS symbols. Use a key to find the meaning of symbols.
STAGE 2	Know that there is a variety of symbolic representations, abbreviations, pictures, words, signs, colour.	Draw a plan of a house using symbols to represent furniture. Use a key. Recognise OS symbols and be able to locate on map, cross reference to key.
STAGE 3	Know term 'legend'. Recognise that different maps serving specific purposes use symbols accordingly.	Through lots of experience with OS symbols use and read OS maps.
STAGE 4	To be familiar with all OS symbols on the range of maps. The conventional signs from 1:50,000 can be used as reference in map reading 'Master Maps' p. 30.	Able to describe an area both urban and rural using symbols, key and relief features. Able to give a written description of a grid square of an OS map.

Build up OS symbols systematically over 4 stages of development

The world around us is full of symbolic representations and the vast majority of children have no difficulty in assimilating such symbols and acting upon them. Even pre-school children recognise the red and green figures at a Pelican crossing and understand the message conveyed. Symbols are all around us and are part of all pupils' lives. Traffic lights, toilet doors, advertising logos are obvious examples of the world of symbols.

Starting Points

Children should be encouraged to draw their own symbols for different features around the school/classroom. A variety of symbols may emerge for the door to the headteacher's room. (Staff should not be encouraged to participate — symbolic representation can be a subversive activity!) Pupils should discuss and compare the various symbols produced with a view to agreeing on the one which seems most appropriate.

Notes on Worksheets

Symbols 1 tackles the thorny problem for some pupils that a symbol is a representation *not* a picture. Thus all telephones, irrespective of size, colour or shape can be represented by a common symbol. Extensions to this idea can be developed by cutting old catalogues and sorting into sets. Collages can be built up which are displayed under pupil-designed symbols.

Once pupils accept the notion of shared meaning and symbolic consistency they will come to the realisation that the symbol for an orchard on an OS Landranger map of Wales is the same as on an OS Landranger map of Kent.

Early exposure to OS symbols is desirable. Ideally pupils should come to internalise and remember them through regular contact. It is a worthwhile exercise for pupils to have their own 'symbols book' which they complete whenever they meet a symbol. These might be subdivided into e.g. Road signs, Land features, Services, Buildings etc.

Symbols 2 introduces a limited number of OS symbols and asks the children to match them to the drawings. There is also a cross-reference to page 30 of 'Discover Maps'.

Symbols 3 is designed to be fun for children who are often fascinated by secret messages and codes — there is a great deal of extension work which can be developed from this. Pupils can devise their own codes and share them with a few others, stressing confidentiality or they can devise a code shared by the whole class. There is also potential in exploring international codes — flags on ships, morse etc.

Symbols 4 Should be seen as an exemplar for what can be produced in your own school. The stress is still on pupils designing suitable symbols. A school which really sees the need to develop this area should have symbolic labelling throughout the building so that all pupils recognise the value of the exercise.

In order to complete **Symbols 5** pupils will need to have the associated skills of using two figure grid references and a key. The worksheet cross refers them to symbol sheets in the Pupil textbook. It is possible to photocopy the grid and for teachers to add their own task to those included on **Symbols 5**. In this way other symbols can be introduced and different locations using the co-ordinates can be identified.

Pupils can design their own symbols.

WORKSHEET	SKILLS INVOLVED	SKILLS PRACTISED IN	
		BOOK 1	BOOK 2
1 Making Sets	Sorting into sets Ability to select the correct symbol	Preparation	
2 Matching symbols and pictures	Selecting symbols Drawing symbols Referring to key	p. 10 p. 28/29	p. 2/3
3 Secret codes using symbols	Code interpretation Writing messages in symbols	p. 28/29	p. 28/29
4 School symbols	Selecting appropriate symbols Using a key Designing symbols	p. 18 p. 19	p. 12 p. 23
5 Using OS symbols	Using OS symbols Using a legend Locating symbols accurately on map	p. 11 p. 30/31	p. 18 p. 23 p. 30/31

Symbols 1   Sorting sets

1 Cut out the pictures below. Make 4 sets.

2 Cut out the symbols.

3 Put the correct symbol with each set.

4 Stick the sets and symbols onto paper.

© Collins Educational: Harrisons/OS Resource Book ▶ You may photocopy this page for use in the classroom ◀

Symbols 2   Matching symbols and pictures

When you draw a map you need to use a code of signs so that you can put lots of things on it. Sometimes we call these signs SYMBOLS.

1 Above are lots of pictures and symbols. Can you match them? Complete the chart.

Picture	Symbol	Description
A	3	Campsite
B		
C		
D		
E		
F		

2 On the back of this worksheet draw pictures for each of these symbols.

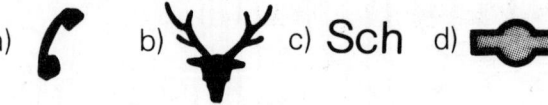

a)   b)   c) Sch   d)

3 Draw the symbols for

a) Post Office   b) Caravan site

c) Lake   d) Marsh

(Use page 30 of 'Discover Maps with OS' to help you)

Symbols 3   Secret codes using symbols

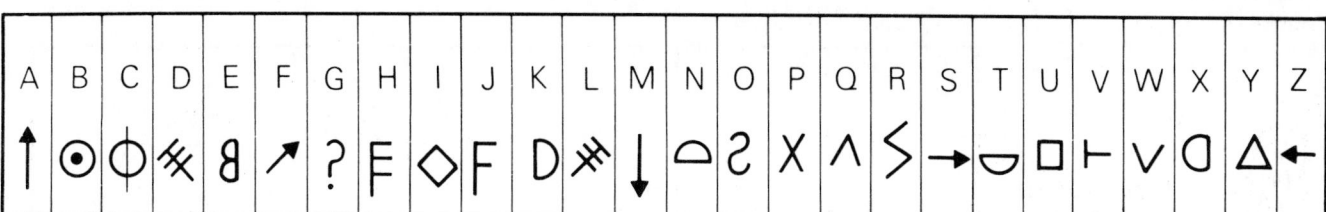

1 What is the symbol for   A _____ N _____ E _____ Z _____ L _____

2 What is the letter for   ⌽ _____ ? _____ ⚹ _____ ⌒ _____ △ _____

3 Write the secret code for

My   name   is   _____

_____ ___   _____

I   live   at   _____

_____ ___   _____

4 What does this message say?

⌒S↓SSSS2V   ◇→   ↑   →⌽FSS⚹   FS⚹◇⚹↑△

_____ ___ _ _____ _____

5 Write a secret message to say what you would do.

_____

_____

6 Ask a friend to crack the code.

_____

_____

Now answer these questions using the code.

Who is your best friend? _____

What is your favourite food? _____

What are your hobbies? _____

7 Send a secret message to a friend using the symbol code.

Symbols in School

Boys toilets

Girls toilets

Library

Caretaker

Corridor

Main entrance

Classroom

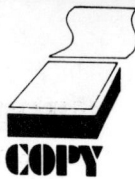

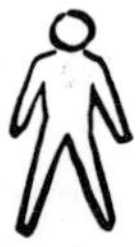

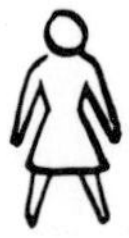

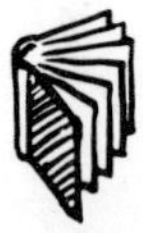

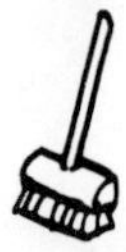

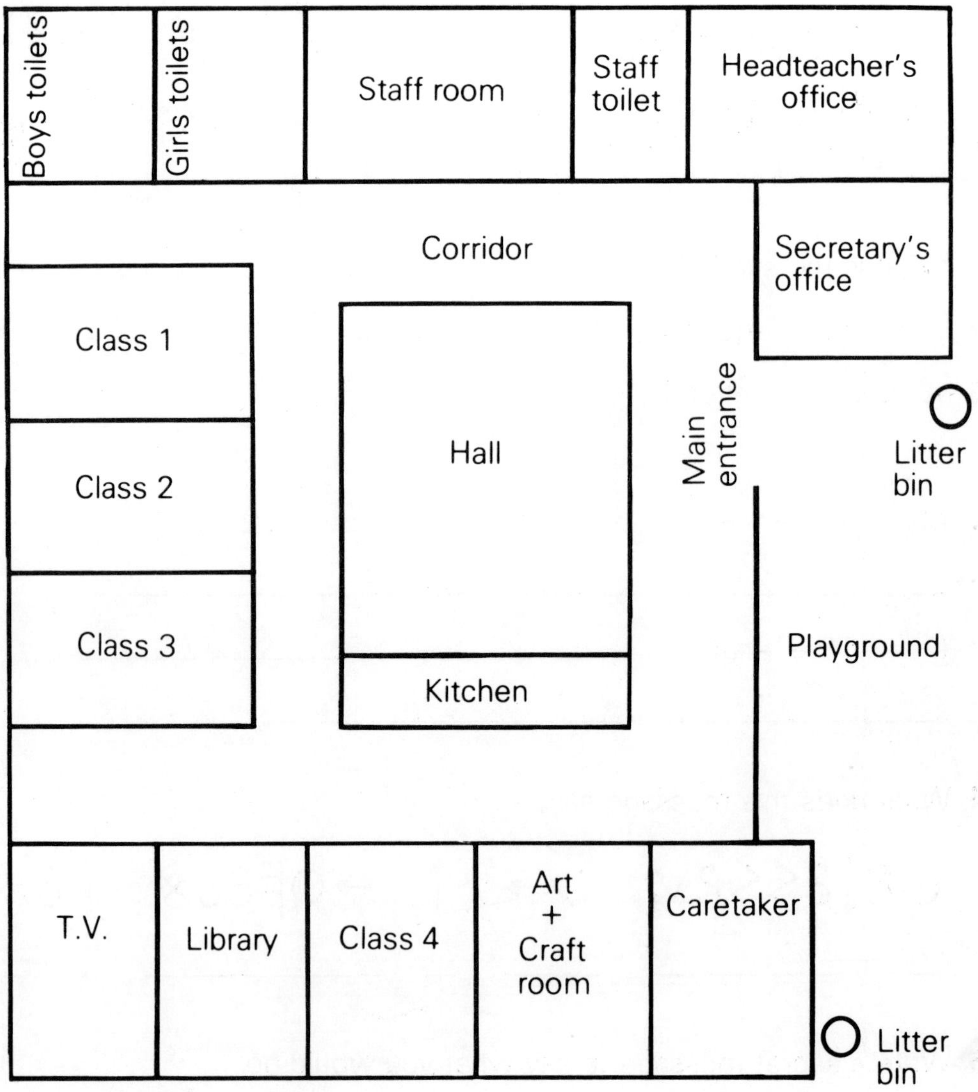

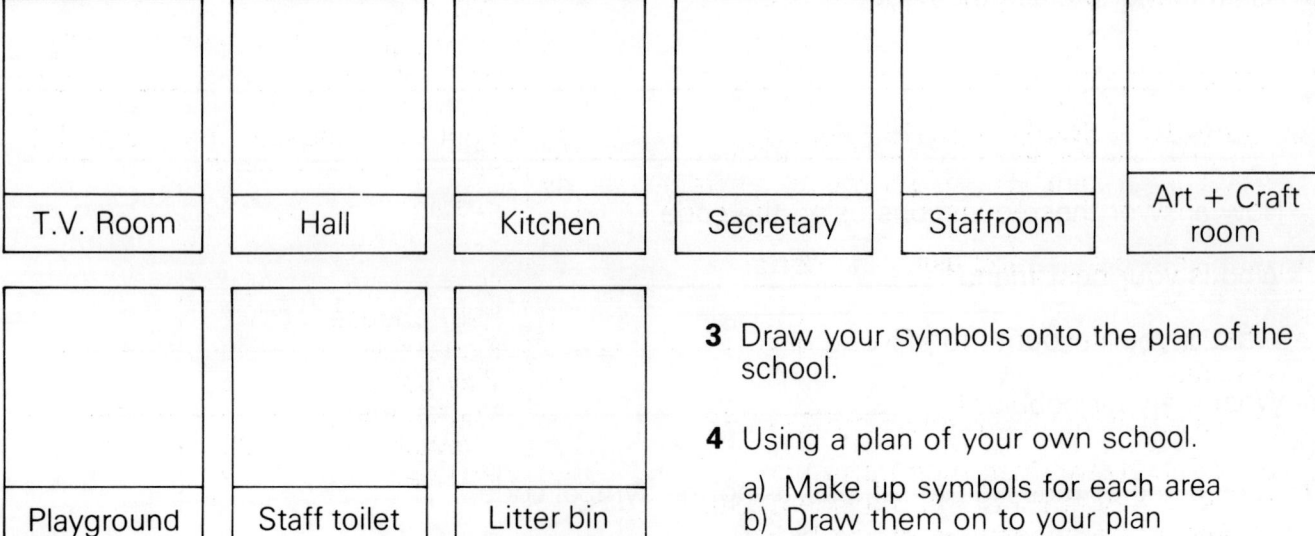

1 Draw the symbols in the correct area of the school.

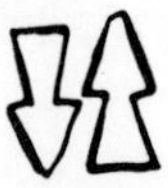

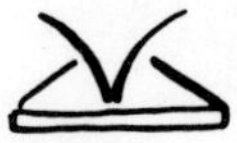

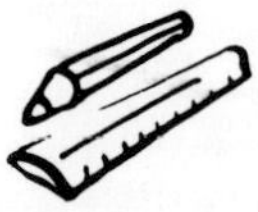

2 Now make suitable symbols for

T.V. Room	Hall	Kitchen	Secretary	Staffroom	Art + Craft room
Playground	Staff toilet	Litter bin			

3 Draw your symbols onto the plan of the school.

4 Using a plan of your own school.

a) Make up symbols for each area
b) Draw them on to your plan

Symbols 5   Using OS symbols

Use the 'Signs and Symbols' on page 30 in 'Discover Maps with OS' to help you.

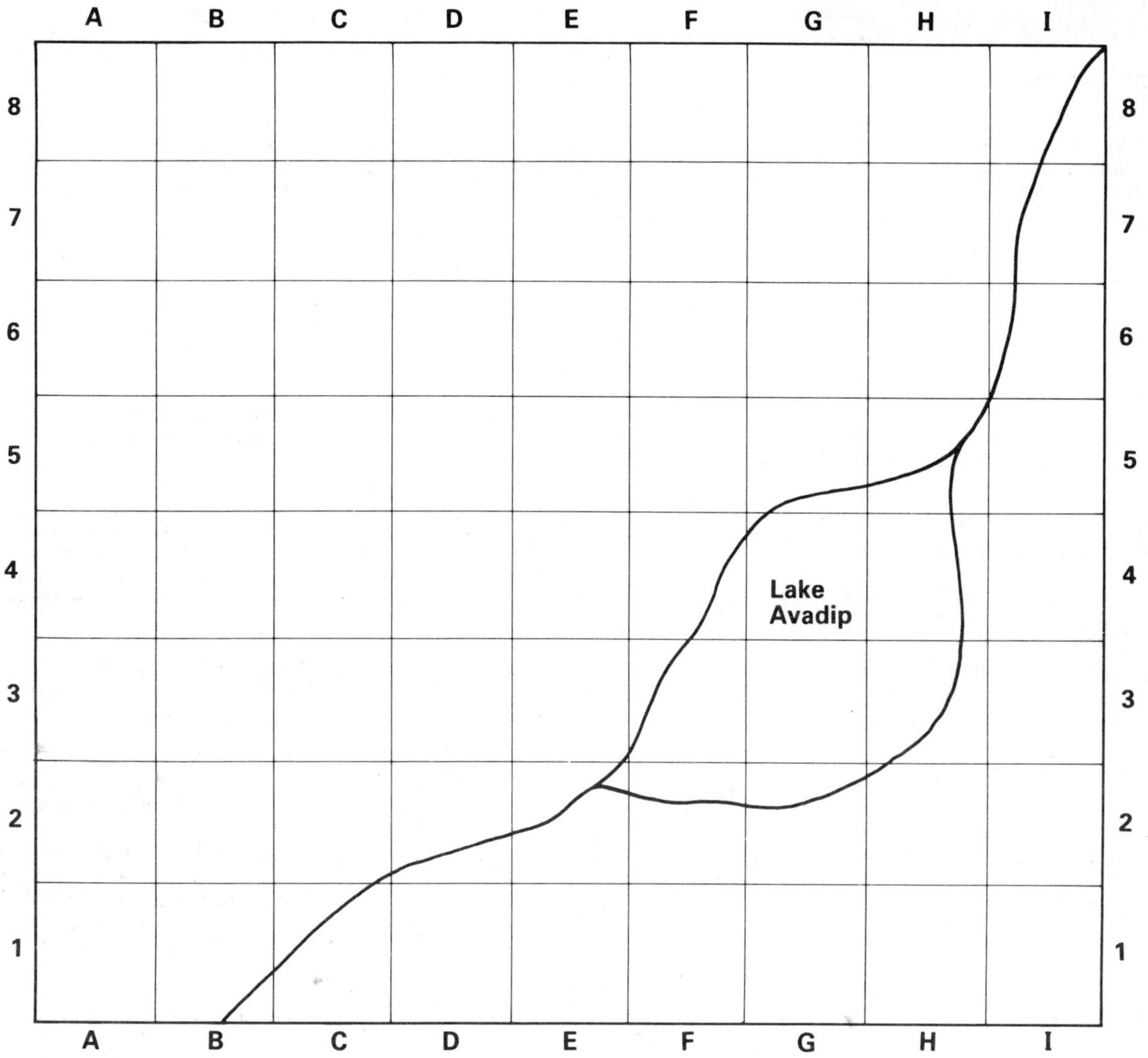

Legend

	Bus station	Picnic site	Coniferous wood
Motorway	Campsite	Viewpoint	Church with tower
Secondary road	Golf course	Wildlife park	Public house
Path	Parking	Footbridge	Information Centre

Lake Avadip is a famous holiday centre.

You will understand why when you complete the map.

1 Complete the Legend using the correct symbols.

2 Put the symbols in the following grid squares.

  a) A straight motorway runs from A3 to H8.

  b) A Secondary Road runs from the motorway at E6 to the lakeside at G5. And in the opposite direction to B8.

  c) A Footbridge crosses the river at I 7.

  d)

Feature	Grid
Golf course	B3
Public house	G2
Picnic site	H5
Viewpoint	E2
Church with tower	D5
Parking	D3

© Collins Educational: Harrisons/OS Resource Book ▶ You may photocopy this page for use in the classroom ◀

Direction

BASIC IDEAS

Need for direction.
Why and how directions are given.
Bearings and direction.

	TARGETS FOR CHILDREN	
	TO KNOW	BE ABLE TO DO
STAGE 1	His/her way round school, location of classes etc. Directional language, e.g. left/right, near/far, nearer/further, in front/behind, more/less than, along, stop/start. The Cardinal Points of the compass introduced.	Give directions using directional language. Draw a simple map. Follow a large scale local map, journey to school. Give directions using cardinal points. Able to replicate a sequence of directions given by the teacher orally, pictorially and in written form.
STAGE 2	Reinforce cardinal points Directional language, e.g. beyond, rear, at the end of, opposite, continue along, advance, reach, pass, return.	Align a map with features of classroom/local area. To use a compass. To give directions using directional language.
STAGE 3	The intermediate points of the compass. Directional vocabulary, e.g. due north, parallel to, adjacent to, branch off.	Basic orienteering using an 8 point compass. Align local maps to compass. To direct a group of children from one point on a map to another using directional vocabulary.
STAGE 4	An 8 point compass. Bearings. Ensure directional language covered at previous stages is reinforced. All road features.	Follow and give bearings using directional language. Use a circular protractor accurately. Orienteering. Describe a journey by using directional language and road features, and using terminology of a local and an alternative environment.

Starting Points

As with symbols, pupils already possess a sense of direction which they bring to school with them. They will use their own shorthand for giving and receiving directions — 'past the shops, over the park etc.'.

In schools we are engaged in developing the precision of pupils' directional language both spoken and understood. Some pupils understand direction but have great difficulty in expressing themselves. In this key aspect, more than any other, there is a vital need to provide opportunities for children to verbalise their thoughts and to practise giving and hearing directional language.

Using the Worksheets

If significant development is to take place pupils will need to be clear about left and right.

Direction 1 is designed to identify children who lack this understanding. A policy of using left/right language in a variety of locations and situations is desirable. Instructional language in P.E. can lay stress on movement to left and right. Classroom directions can be used similarly — 'collect the papers from the desk to the left of the board'.

Practical Activities

Make some sample sets of directional language cards.

backwards	forwards	right	left
↓	↑	→	←

Children can play simple board games using a die and the cards — 'forward 5', '6 to the left', etc. The same principle can be applied to a further set of cards which will become part of the teacher's armoury.

North	South	East	West
↑	↓	→	←

Amusing grid squares can be designed and drawn by pupils and used in similar games.

25 is an ideal number of squares. 30 direction cards are shuffled and used. After 4 throws pupils can compare whether they are in positive/negative positions.

A further development is to produce directional cards which give intermediate points of the compass.

Direction 2 substitutes N.S.E.W. for left/right. The worksheet also reinforces 'colour key' work.

Direction 3 continues with N.S.E.W. but places the onus far more on the child to play and describe a route.

Direction 4 completes the simple directional work by offering practice in the intermediate points of NW, NE, SW, SE. The final question on the sheet combines cardinal and intermediate points.

Direction 5 introduces bearings. It is sensible to approach this work at the same time that a 360° protractor is being used in maths. The practical use of the protractor in geographical work makes it much more meaningful for pupils.

Clearly a supply of compasses would be a great asset. Even a basic compass provides a 360° dial along with cardinal points.

The worksheet requires pupils to give directional information in two forms — by cardinal points and by degrees.

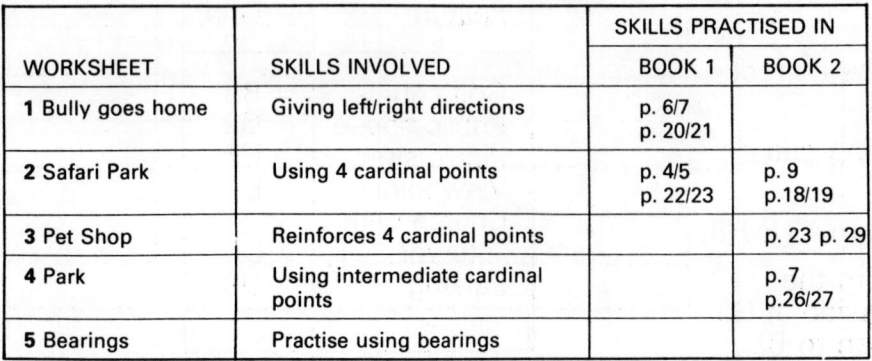

WORKSHEET	SKILLS INVOLVED	SKILLS PRACTISED IN	
		BOOK 1	BOOK 2
1 Bully goes home	Giving left/right directions	p. 6/7 p. 20/21	
2 Safari Park	Using 4 cardinal points	p. 4/5 p. 22/23	p. 9 p.18/19
3 Pet Shop	Reinforces 4 cardinal points		p. 23 p. 29
4 Park	Using intermediate cardinal points		p. 7 p.26/27
5 Bearings	Practise using bearings		

Direction 1   Bully goes home

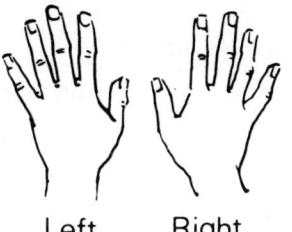
Left   Right

Plan of Oxtail Farm

1 Complete the chart.

Left	Centre	Right
Kennels	Pigs	Cows
	Farmhouse	
	Kennels	
	Farm machinery	
	Garden	
	Hens	

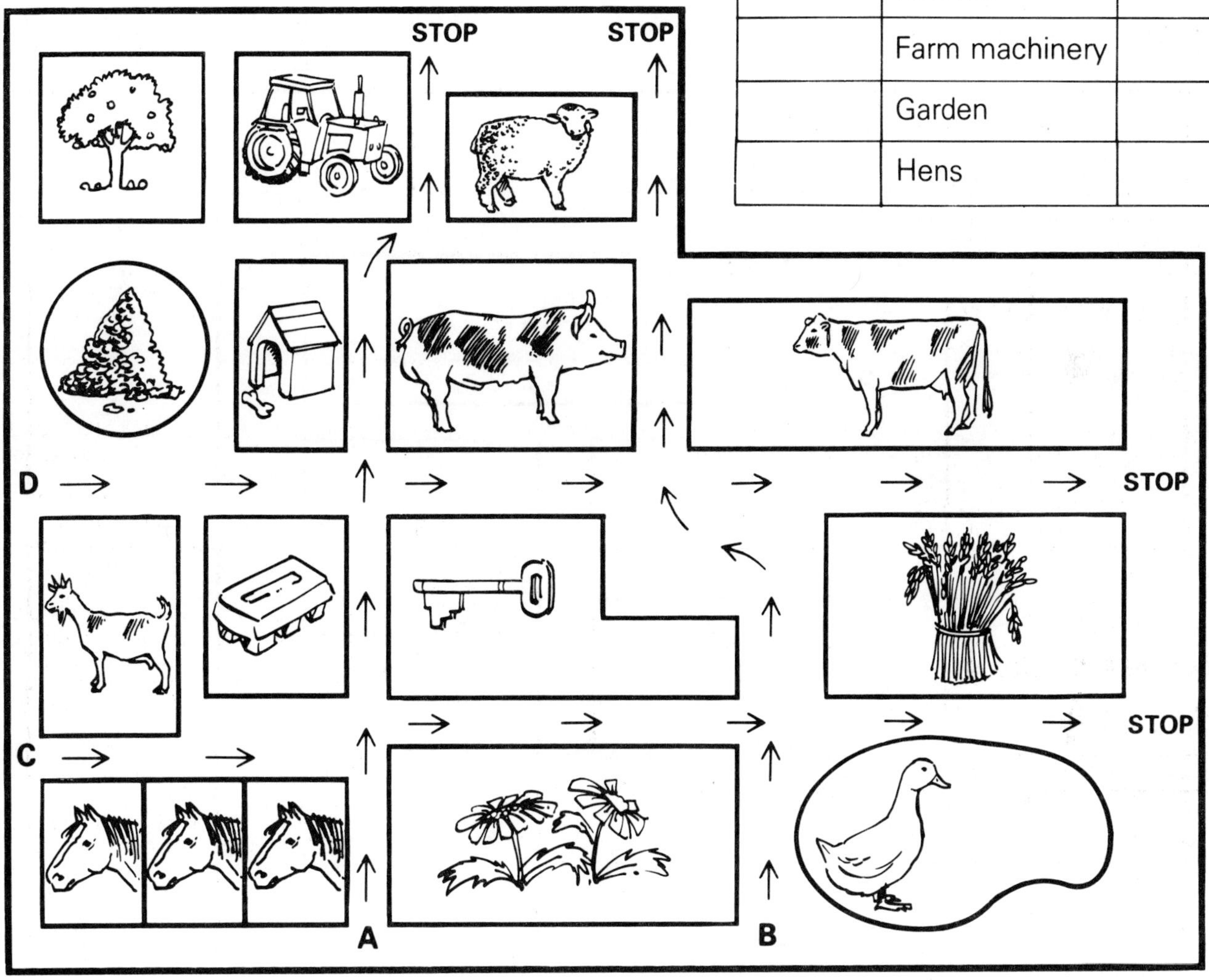

key			
	Pond		Pigs
	Stables		Cows
	Garden		Goats
	Barn		Farm machinery
	Farmhouse		Orchard
	Hens		Lambs
	Silo		Kennels

2 Follow the routes.
List what you see on your left and right.

	Left	Right
A		
B		

	Left	Right
C		
D		

© Collins Educational: Harrisons/OS Resource Book ▶ You may photocopy this page for use in the classroom ◀

Direction 2   Safari Park

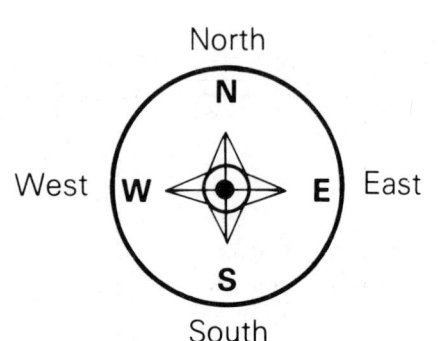

Colour Key	S	Snake	E	Elephant
	M	Monkey	G	Giraffe
T	Toilet	B	Bird	P	Picnic area
K	Kangaroo	L	Lion	F	Fountain
R	Rhinoceros	Ti	Tiger	O	Office

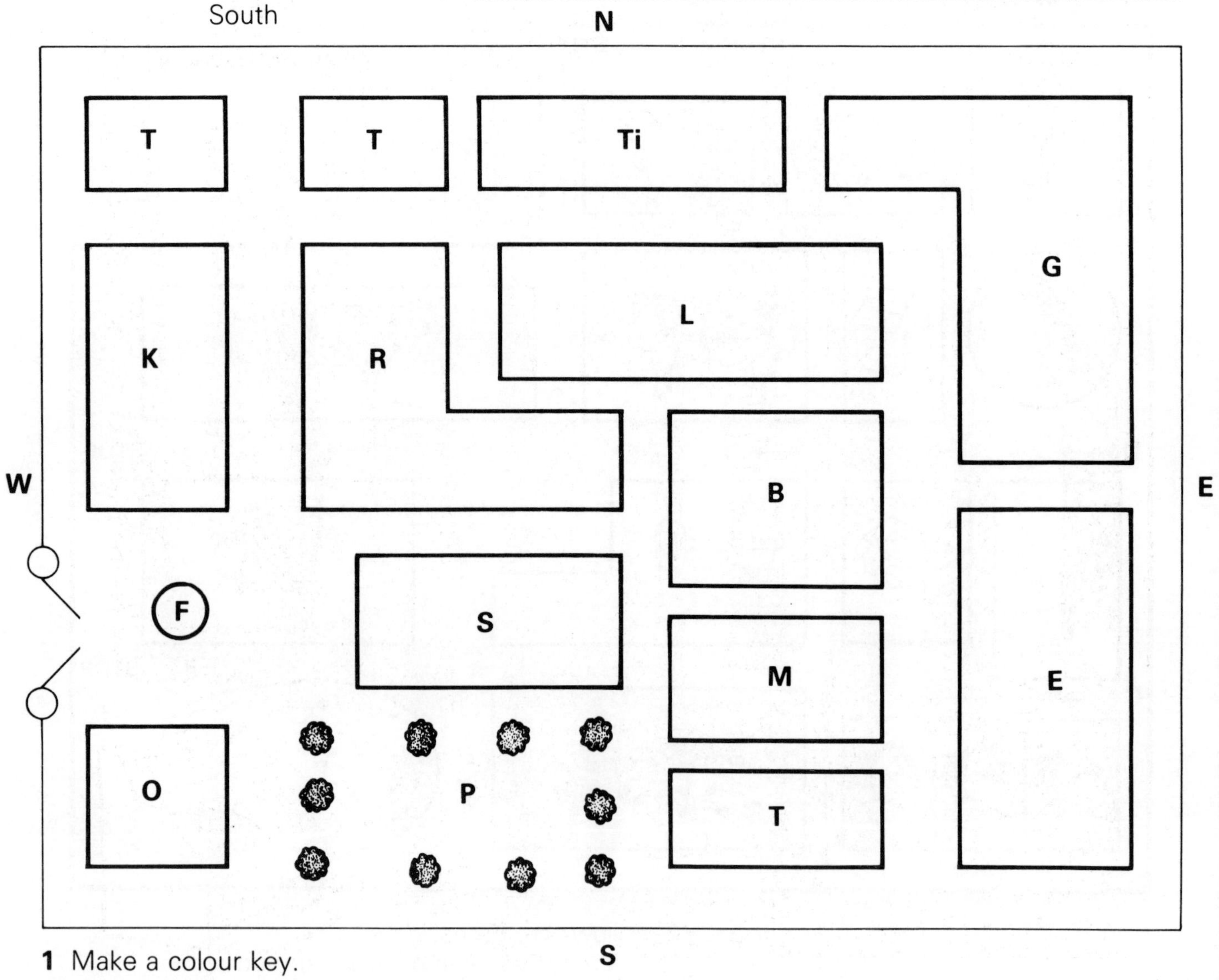

1 Make a colour key.

2 Colour the plan of the zoo to match the key.

3 The tigers are NORTH of the Lions. What is NORTH of
   a) The Monkeys _____
   b) The Office _____
   c) The Elephants _____

4 What is EAST of
   a) The Monkeys _____
   b) The Office _____
   c) The Lions _____

5 What is WEST of
   a) The Rhinoceros _____
   b) The Snakes _____
   c) The Birds _____

6 What is SOUTH of
   a) The Birds _____
   b) The Monkeys _____
   c) The Snakes _____

Direction 3   Pet Shop

Tina wants to buy a new pet.
Tina follows these directions to the puppy:

START [A] East, South, West, South.

1. Now write the directions to the other pets on the chart. Use the letters E, S, W and N.

2. Make a second chart to show the directions from each pet to the till where Tina will pay.

Pet	Start	Directions
Puppy	A	E, S, W, S
Cat	A	
Rabbit	A	
Bird	A	
Fish	A	
Mouse	B	
Snake	B	
Tortoise	B	

Direction 4   In the Park

1 North West is halfway between North and West.
   a) North East is _____
   b) South East is _____
   c) South West is _____

KEY

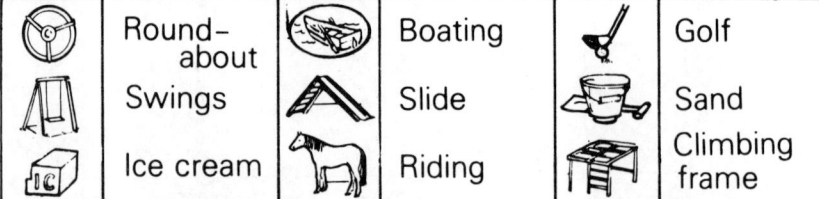

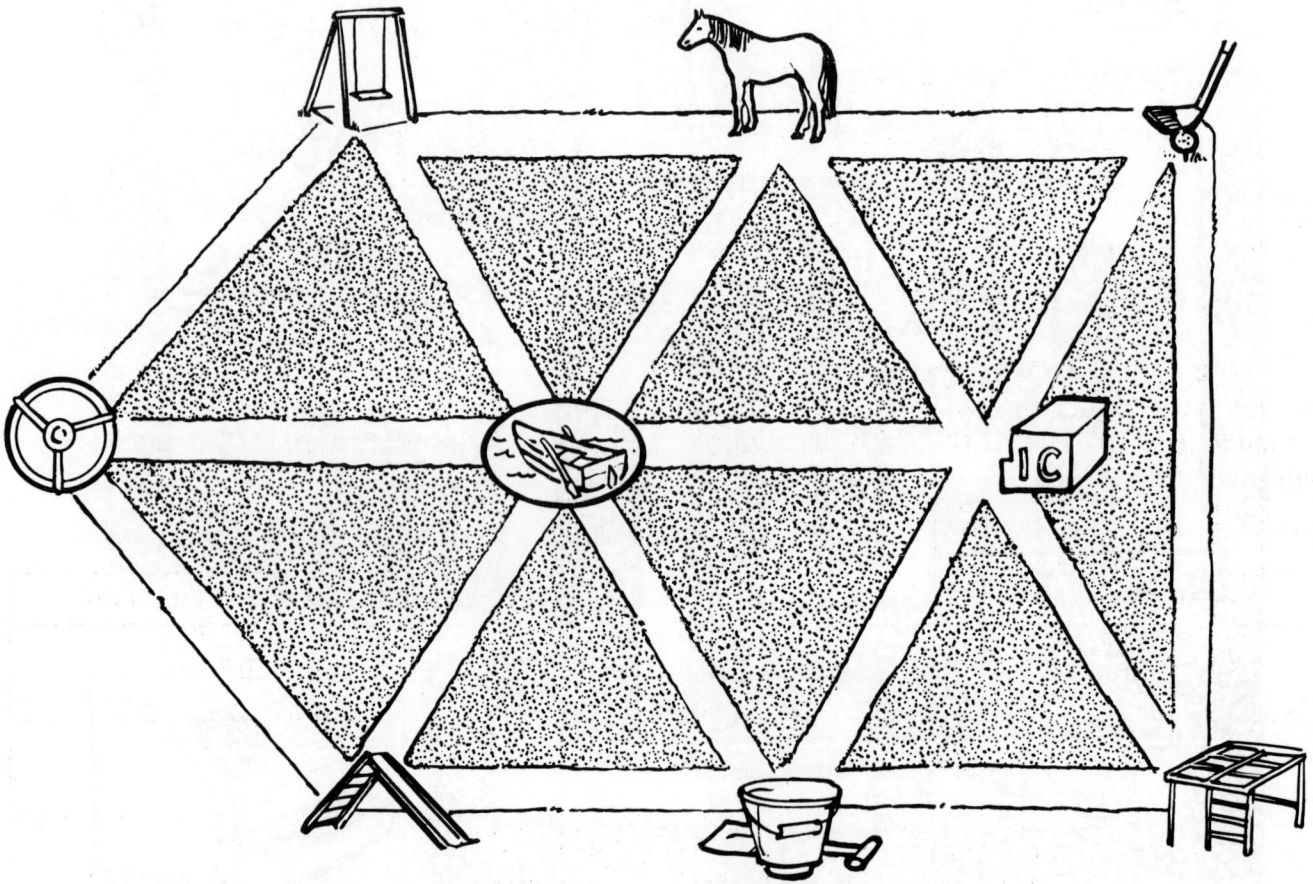

2 Starting from the boating lake each time.
   In which direction would you walk to
   a) The swings _____
   b) Riding _____
   c) The sand _____
   d) The slide _____
   e) The roundabout _____
   f) The ice cream _____

3 Complete the chart.

Start	Stop	Direction
Slide	Boating	N.E.
Ice cream	Roundabout	
Riding	Boating	
Ice cream	Sand	
Climbing frame	Golf	
Golf	Ice cream	
Sand	Ice cream	
Roundabout	Boating	
Sand	Boating	

Direction 5   Using Bearings

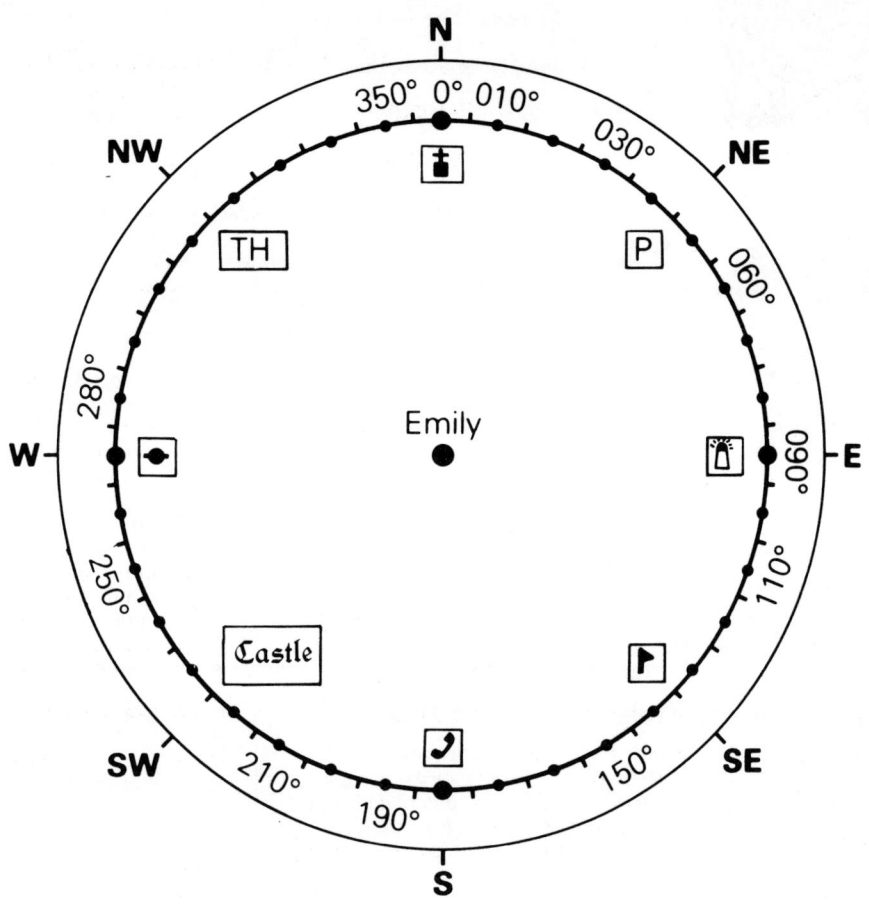

You can give directions more accurately by using bearings.
The circle is divided into 360°. Each object around the circle can be identified by the number of degrees.

Complete the chart.

Feature	Symbol	Bearing in Degrees	Compass direction
Lighthouse	🔦	090°	EAST

Scale

BASIC IDEA
Understand and interpret a variety of scales.

	TARGETS FOR CHILDREN	
	TO KNOW	BE ABLE TO DO
STAGE 1	To be familiar with the term 'scale'. To know that objects are drawn in relation to each other.	Observe and estimate lengths. Able to draw a sketch map from a larger one. Able to use arbitrary measurement e.g. 1cm:2 paces. Basic introduction to recording procedures.
STAGE 2	Know and use the terms plan, scale, reduce, enlarge. Recognise the need for accurate measurement.	Observe and record reasonably accurately. Use ½ scale 1:2. Use ¼ scale 1:4. Reduce and enlarge plans. Use string to measure routes.
STAGE 3	Know 1:2 1:4 OS 1:1,250 OS 1:2,500 OS 1:10,000	Able to estimate reasonably accurately before measuring. Able to choose appropriate scale and record accurately with relatively little assistance.
STAGE 4	Know OS 1:25,000 OS 1:50,000	Define scale accurately. Able to choose appropriate scale in map making. Use a linear scale. Experience a variety of scales. Use precise measurement.

Starting Points

We should always look for what the child can already do. A basic conceptual understanding will be found in most children. At its simplest level this can be seen when a child draws a parent, friend, house, dog or whatever on paper. The visual representation may not be particularly lifelike *but* it fits on the paper! The very act of drawing something from observation or memory and reducing the subject so that it fits on the paper provided is a practical demonstration of the use of scale.

The child is aware that the representation on the paper is a miniature version of a much larger real-life object. It is on this foundation that we must build. We want the child, eventually, to recognise that accurate representation smaller than life-size must be in proportion, i.e. the parts of the subject ought to be in the same ratio on the page as in life. Clearly in this book we are specifically concerned with scale in relation to maps and mapwork. The principle is the same. Maps provide a two-dimensional representation of a three-dimensional world. This representation is reduced and the reduction has to be consistent. Precise measurement of the object to be mapped will be reflected in the precise measurement of the resultant plan.

There need to be opportunities for children to experience drawing to scale so that they will better understand the process of map making.

It is desirable to begin with cm² paper. The motor skills for accurate drawing may not be present if this is begun with younger children and the inability to draw accurately can inhibit the objective. Squared paper helps build confidence at the outset. The emphasis is on counting squares in these early stages.

There ought also to be a clear strategy for first hand observation of a variety of objects/scenes at different scales and for discussion of the choice of scale.

WORKSHEET	SKILLS INVOLVED	
1 Castle	Simple enlargement 1:2 representation	
2 Clown	1:2 enlargement complicated shape	
3 Kitchen Planner	Using 1:25 scale pre-drawn shapes	
4 Bedroom Designer	Using 1:25 scale Drawing furniture to scale Measuring accurately	Children meet many different scales of map in both mapping books. The authors feel it is important that children develop the concept of scale systematically from a simple level. These worksheets are designed as preparation for the books.
5 Routes to Scale	Using 1:50 linear scale Measuring routes accurately	

Using the Worksheets

Scale 1 is a straightforward enlargement exercise. Once completed there is a need for discussion about the relationship between Pictures A and B. The objective is an understanding that in all respects 'B' is twice the dimension of 'A' — and that the size difference is consistent.

Pupils can then work in pairs in order to develop this activity. Child 'A' draws an object on 1 cm or 2 cm squared paper. Child 'B' either reduces or enlarges the partner's drawing.

Scale 2 continues the theme but adds a degree of difficulty by introducing curved as well as straight lines. This is an important step. All shapes, no matter how complex, need to be reduced to the appropriate scale. Again children working in pairs can develop this theme.

Once the pupils have internalised the process of reducing and enlarging it is necessary to change the ratios from 1:2 to 1:4 etc.

Scale 3 moves to a more concrete application of the principles of scale:— Planning a Kitchen. The measurement is not carried out by the pupils as all dimensions and shapes are given but the challenge is to make decisions about location, relative sizes, available space and suitability.

Scale 4 places the onus on the pupils to measure accurately, draw the furniture and then place it in appropriate settings. The focus must be on accurate measurement and well drawn right angles.

The teacher can develop this theme by
a) providing basic dimensions and asking pupils to design other rooms
b) involving the pupils in drawing an accurate scale plan of the classroom and its contents.
c) placing the onus on the pupils to carry out their own measurements of a room at home which they may then re-design.

Throughout this work discussion of the *appropriate* scale is vital. When the children work on their own plans/designs they should be encouraged to choose paper of an appropriate size and a scale which is workable.

Scale 5 introduces a separate aspect of scale — distance. Routes are measured using string (whenever possible avoid wool, elastic etc. as the stretch element distorts the accuracy). The string is then measured and the scale used to convert the reading to actual distance travelled.

Extension work can focus on the classroom and pupil's own routes. The group will need to agree an appropriate scale. It is important that the children always have the chance to estimate before measuring. Charts for recording should have an estimation column. It is only through constantly observing, estimating and accurately measuring that pupils will truly develop the skills and understanding we hope for them.

Scale 1   The Castle

A

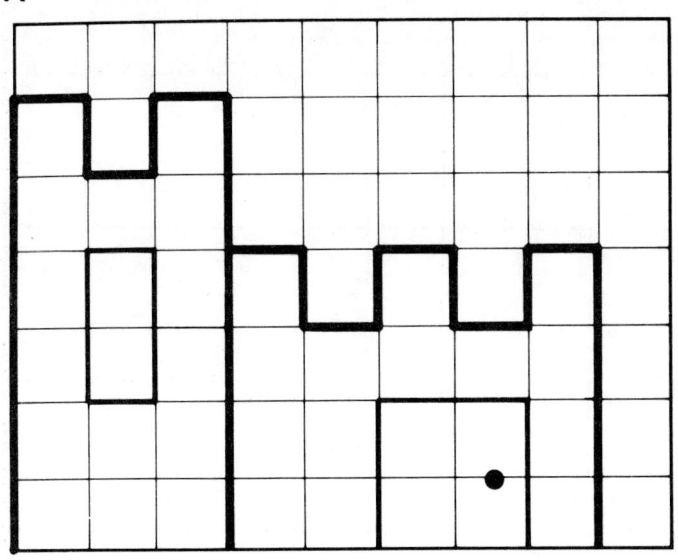

1 Draw the castle on Grid B.

2 Complete the chart.

	Castle A		Castle B	
	Height	Width	Height	Width
Door	2cm	2cm		
Window				
Tower				

B

Scale 2 The Clown

1. Draw the clown on Grid B.
2. Add to both clowns
   a) buttons b) belt c) funny face
3. Colour both clowns with patterns. Make sure the patterns are in the right square on each clown.
4. Complete the chart.

	Clown A	Clown B
Height of clown		
Length of foot		
Height of hat		
Width of shoulders		

5. What do you notice about the measurements in A and B?

_____

_____

_____

B

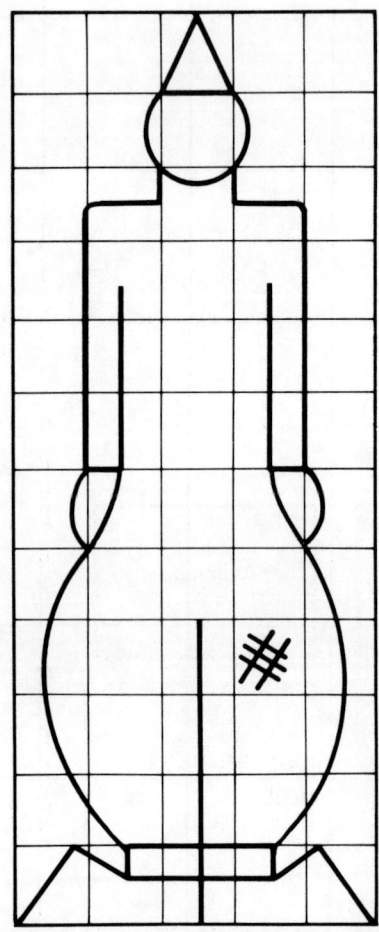

A

28 © Collins Educational: Harrisons/OS Resource Book ▶ You may photocopy this page for use in the classroom ◀

Scale 3   Kitchen Planner

Cut out the kitchen furniture and choose where to put it on the plan.

You may need to cut out more shapes if you want more than one single unit for example. You may also want to add table, chairs, breakfast bar etc.

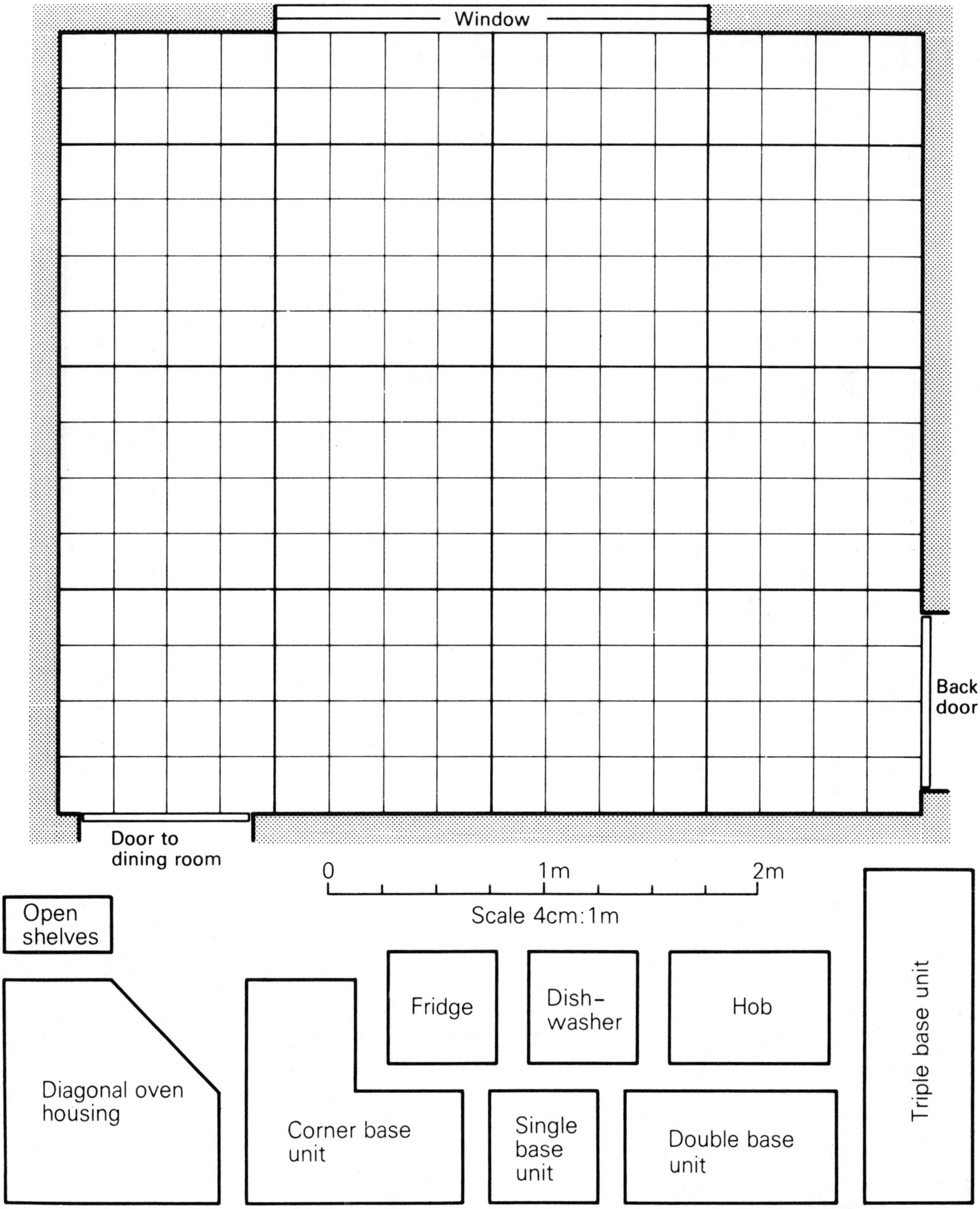

Window

Back door

Door to dining room

0   1m   2m

Scale 4cm:1m

Open shelves

Diagonal oven housing

Corner base unit

Fridge

Dish-washer

Single base unit

Hob

Double base unit

Triple base unit

Compare your plan with that of a friend. Which do you like best?

© Collins Educational: Harrisons/OS Resource Book ▶ You may photocopy this page for use in the classroom ◀

Scale 4 Bedroom Designer

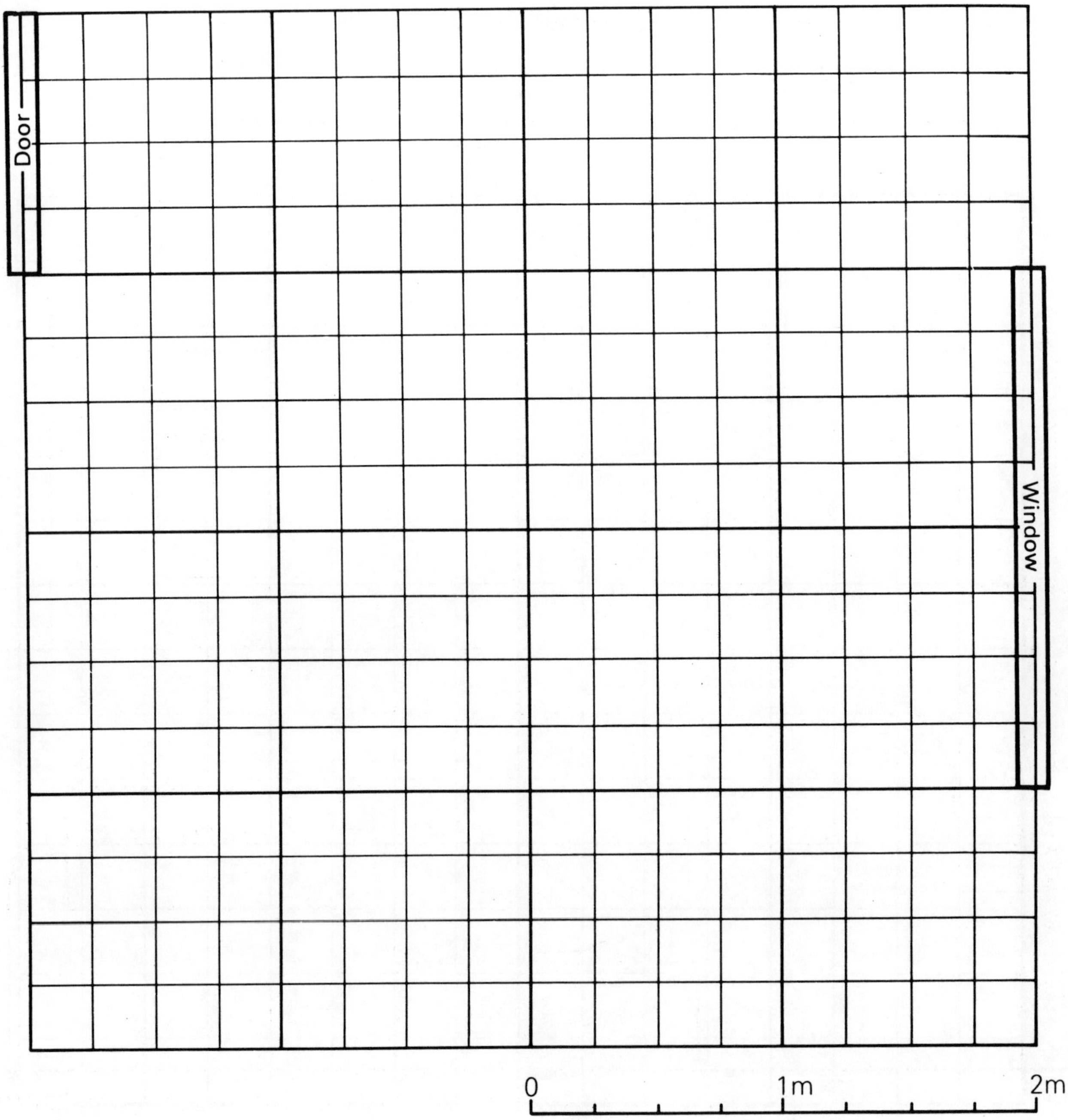

0   1m   2m

Scale 4cm:1m

1. You are going to design a bedroom. Decide which furniture best suits you.
2. Draw each piece to scale using 1cm² paper.
3. Arrange them on your plan.
4. When you are happy with the design stick them down.
5. Are there pieces of furniture not on the chart that you would like? Draw them to scale and stick them on your plan.
6. Draw or paint a large picture of your designer bedroom. Design all the soft furnishings like wallpaper, curtains etc.

Furniture Dimensions		
Item	Width	Length
Bed	1m	2m
Wardrobe	75cm	2m
Dressing table	75cm	1.5m
Bedside cabinet	50cm	50cm
Settee	75cm	1.5m
Chair	1m	1m
Small table	75cm	75cm
Stereo	50cm	50cm

Scale 5   Recording to scale

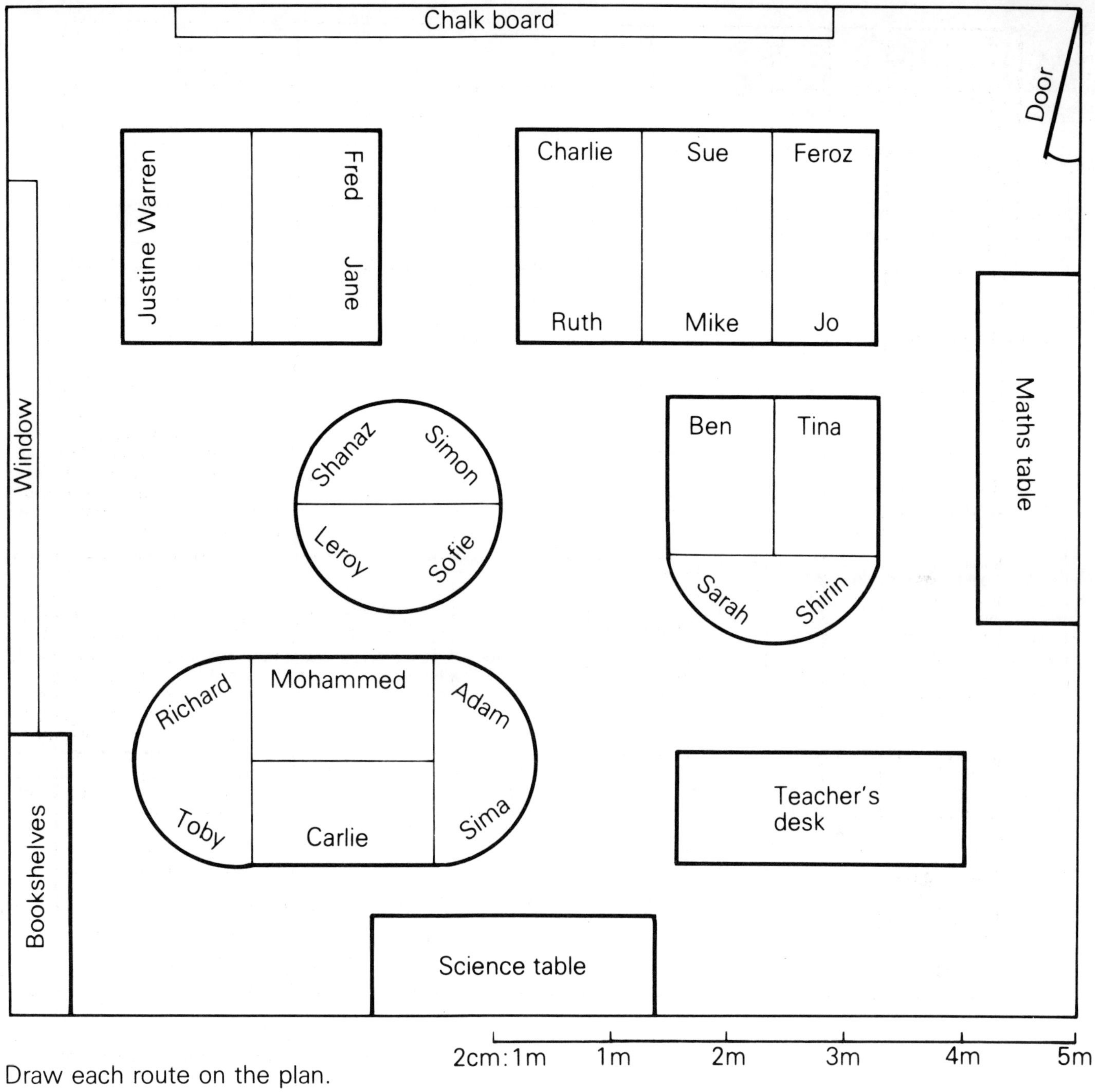

[Classroom plan showing: Chalk board along top, Door in top-right, Window on left, Bookshelves on lower-left, Maths table on right, Teacher's desk, Science table along bottom. Desks with children: Justine/Warren/Fred/Jane (rectangular desk top-left); Charlie/Sue/Feroz/Ruth/Mike/Jo (rectangular desk top-centre); Shanaz/Simon/Leroy/Sofie (round table centre); Ben/Tina/Sarah/Shirin (D-shaped desk centre-right); Richard/Mohammed/Adam/Toby/Carlie/Sima (oval desk lower-centre). Scale bar: 2cm:1m, marked 1m, 2m, 3m, 4m, 5m.]

Draw each route on the plan.

1 Use a piece of string to measure the distance travelled by each child. Complete the chart.

Person	Journey	Distance
Warren	Maths table	9m
Shanaz	Science table	
Ruth	Teacher's desk	
Ben	Teacher's desk	
Sima	Door	
Feroz	Bookshelves	
Tina	Door	
Jo	Window	

2 Every child in the class visits the teacher's desk once. Every child in the class enters through the door and leaves through the door. Draw on the plan these 3 routes for each child. Use 3 different colours.

3 Look at your plan. The busy places in the classroom are where there are the most routes. Draw a red circle around the busy places.

© Collins Educational: Harrisons/OS Resource Book ▶ You may photocopy this page for use in the classroom ◀

Routes

BASIC IDEA
To understand that journeys follow an observable, recordable pattern.

	TARGETS FOR CHILDREN	
	TO KNOW	BE ABLE TO DO
STAGE 1	To know the terms route and journey and to appreciate journeys have purposes and patterns.	To follow a route on a large scale map of the classroom. To draw in routes of several people and identify busy places.
STAGE 2	To reinforce stage 1 and understand and be familiar with routes in the school and in the locality.	To follow routes on a plan of the school. Identify designed routes e.g. paths and actual routes, e.g. short cuts across grass. Examine reasons and solutions. Be able to draw on an appropriate local map own route to school.
STAGE 3	To understand different route systems e.g. one way, dual carriageways, cyclepaths, traffic routes, pedestrian routes etc.	To examine local maps for designed routes. Observations in the local environment of actual routes taken e.g. not crossing at pelican. Think about solutions.
STAGE 4	Understand networks, local pedestrian networks, local bus networks, national route networks. Relate to real world at each level.	Be able to draw on a local map the routes to school of the class. Identify the type of network. Compare with different networks. Empathise with people who have special needs and the hazards presented by lack of consideration to them e.g. people in wheelchairs, senior citizens, those with babies — prams.

Children are already conversant with a wide variety of routes. From an early age they know certain routes which they have walked regularly — to the local shops, to a neighbour or relative, to a friend's home. These routes will be well known to them and many features on the way will be part of their memorised mental map.

In urban areas some routes will belong mainly to childen, particularly on their way to and from school. Children often use narrow back passageways rather than main roads. These may well be traffic free and there they can meet friends.

In rural areas children may use routes which are short-cuts closed to traffic, over footbridges, stiles etc.

In both urban and rural situations most children will have considerable experience of walking to leisure points, friends, playgrounds, parks, swimming baths etc. They will also have experience of routes travelled by bicycle, car and bus. Bicycle routes will generate the best mental maps, because children have to consider where to turn, what they pass, familiar landmarks etc. Car routes may not generate the same degree of recall. Many children may simply sit in the back and ignore their surroundings. This is also true of some bus travel, however the last part of a bus route is usually known, as the child has to be aware of when to alight.

Many teachers ask their pupils to draw their routes from home to school. This is a very varied task which requires different concepts and skills from individual pupils. Consider two pupils given the same task. Pupil A lives 6 houses down the road from school. Pupil B lives 16 km away and travels the first part of the journey by bus, transfers to train and completes the journey on foot from the station, crossing a canal and a dual carriageway on the way. Clearly these are very different tasks and it is impossible to compare the responses of the two children in a meaningful way.

Starting Points

It is worthwhile considering the potential offered by the school and its grounds for route work. All schools should have recommended 'escape routes' in the event of fire. These can be walked and drawn on a school plan. Many schools have policies about the movement of pupils around the premises and these too can be supported by plans of the school (e.g. pupil entrances, keep to the left on corridors etc.).

The play area/grounds also offer great potential. Trails around the yard/grounds can be designed. These will build on directional language and skills. Start with directional arrows and the number of paces leading from one landmark to another. Pupils should be encouraged while on these routes, to look at their surroundings, try to memorise the features passed to left and right and most importantly *in sequence*. The process is *walk, look, remember* and *draw* back in the classroom. This process can be supported by making sketches and notes or even a photographic record.

The same principles should apply to movement in the local environment. A walk from school to library (or church, mosque, market, field etc.) is an opportunity for the development of mental mapping. Pupils can record their journey and try to match their record to real maps back in the classroom. The teacher can provide a photo pack which is out of sequence and challenge the pupils to order it correctly.

Using the Worksheets

Routes 1 — The plan of the school is an imaginary one. Once used it is good practice to provide pupils with a similar plan of their own school (which they might be involved in drawing). Using an own school plan they can design symbols, label the plan and answer questions about routes set either by the teacher or by other pupils.

Routes 2 — The worksheet moves from the school plan to a local environment. Once again by drawing routes on the map children will recognise high density and low density points. This needs to be reinforced as a concept through discussion. The worksheet requires skills and understanding of scale and direction in addition to routes. Once completed a local OS map should be used in a similar way.

Routes 3 — The three maps shown are of scales 1:2500, 1:10,000 and 1:25,000. The early tasks require pupils to draw routes on the worksheet. The later tasks are designed to provide opportunities for pupils to identify differences between maps and their respective contents. Teachers may consider adding extracts from 1:1250 and 1:50,000 OS maps with appropriate tasks for pupils.

WORKSHEET	SKILLS INVOLVED	SKILLS PRACTISED IN	
		BOOK 1	BOOK 2
1 School Journeys	Following a route Accurate measurement Using string to measure Estimation Scale 1:200	p. 6/7	p. 9/10 p. 14/15
2 Local Journeys	Following routes Accurate measurement Using string to measure Scale 1:1000	p. 8/9 p. 20/21 p. 23, 25	p. 18/19 p. 24/25 p. 26/27
3 Choosing the Right Map	Selecting correct map for specific purposes		p. 17 p. 22/23

Routes 1   School Journeys

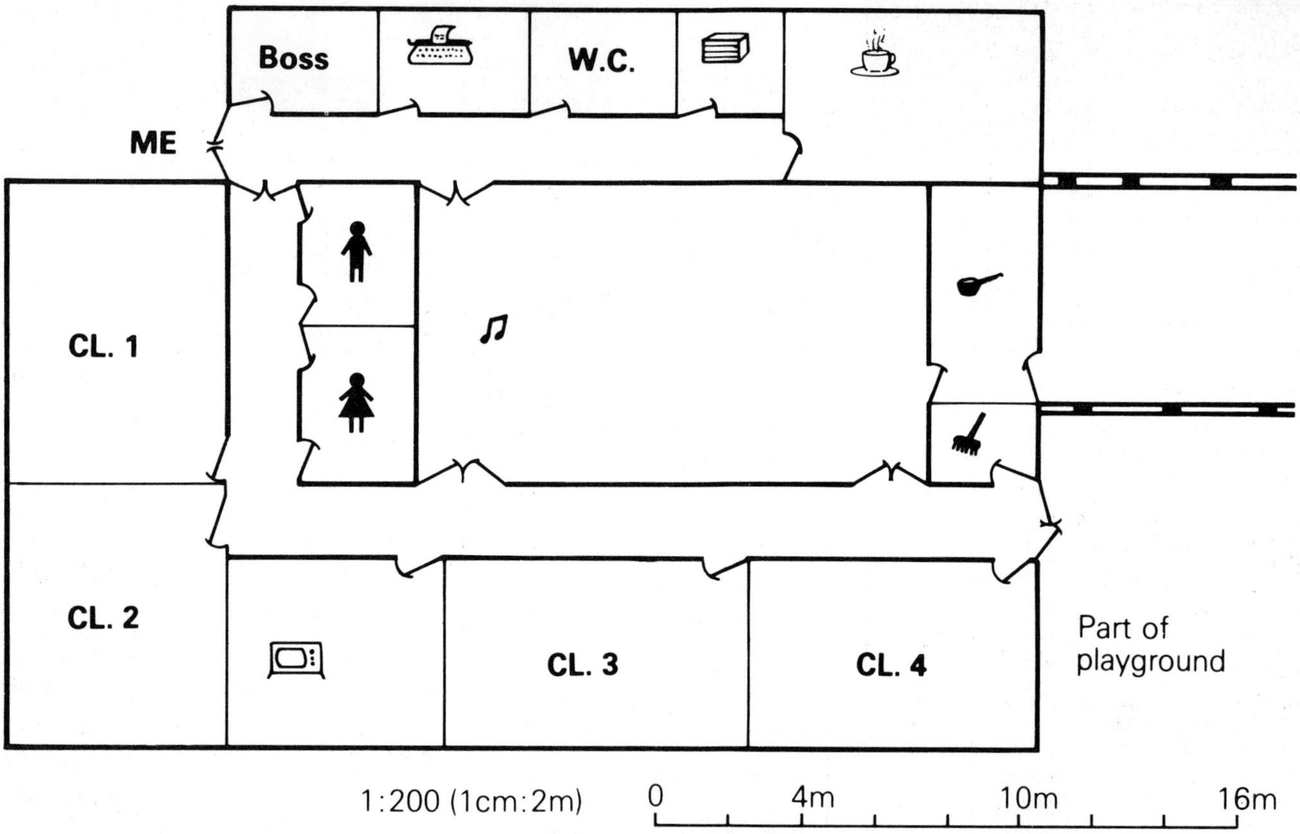

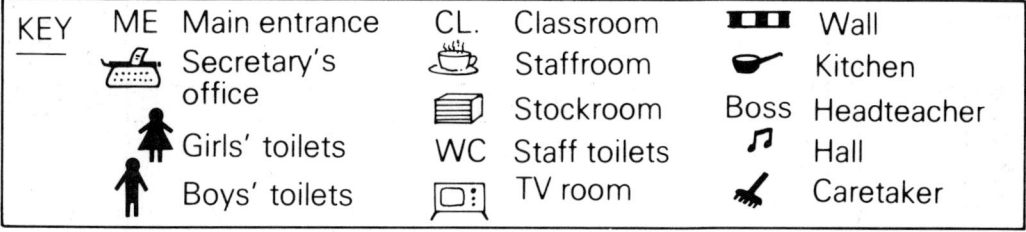

1:200 (1cm:2m)   0   4m   10m   16m

KEY	ME	Main entrance	CL.	Classroom		Wall
—		Secretary's office		Staffroom		Kitchen
				Stockroom	Boss	Headteacher
		Girls' toilets	WC	Staff toilets	♪	Hall
		Boys' toilets		TV room		Caretaker

1 Use a ruler to measure each room. Complete the chart.

Room Symbol	Using a ruler		In real life	
	Width	Length	Width	Length
CL. 1	3cm	4cm	6m	8m
♪				
🧹				
🍳				
👧				

2 Draw in these routes on the plan using different coloured crayons.

Colour	Person	From	To
Red	Cook	Kitchen	Staffroom
Blue	Secretary	Office	T.V. room
Green	Headteacher	Her room	Class 4
Orange	Caretaker	Girls toilets	Stockroom
Purple	Teacher	Playground	Class 1
Yellow	Teacher	Staffroom	Playground

3 a) First estimate how far each person walked.

b) Use a piece of string to measure each route.

Hold the string carefully on each route. Now move carefully to the scale marked on the plan (or a ruler). Check the actual distance.

Complete the chart.

Route	Estimate	String measurement
Red	20m	23m
Blue		
Green		
Orange		
Purple		
Yellow		

© Collins Educational: Harrisons/OS Resource Book ▶ You may photocopy this page for use in the classroom ◀

Routes 2 Local Journeys

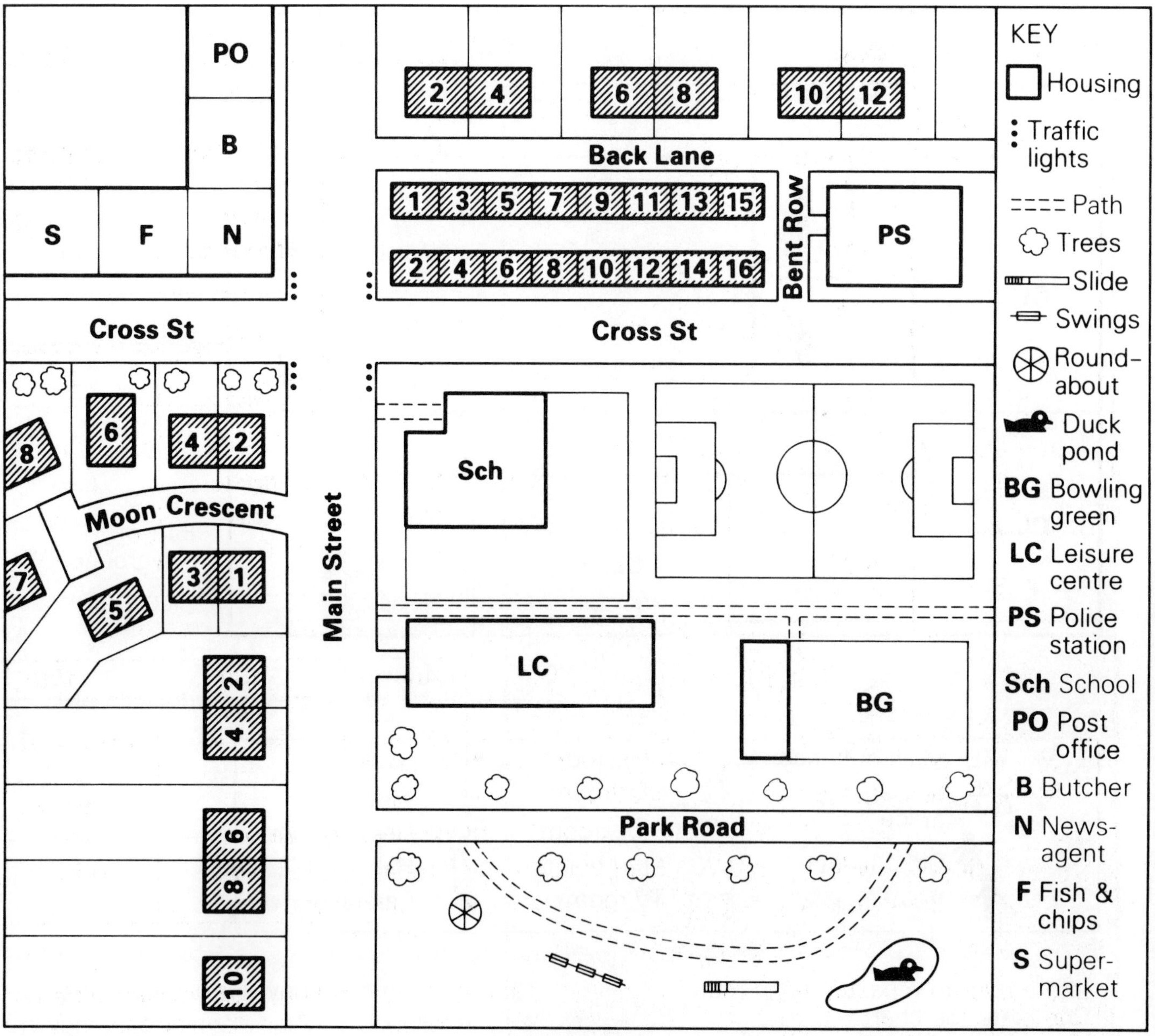

KEY
- ☐ Housing
- ⋮ Traffic lights
- ╌╌╌ Path
- ○ Trees
- ▭▬ Slide
- ▬═ Swings
- ⊕ Roundabout
- 🦆 Duck pond
- **BG** Bowling green
- **LC** Leisure centre
- **PS** Police station
- **Sch** School
- **PO** Post office
- **B** Butcher
- **N** Newsagent
- **F** Fish & chips
- **S** Supermarket

Scale 1:1000 (1cm:10m)

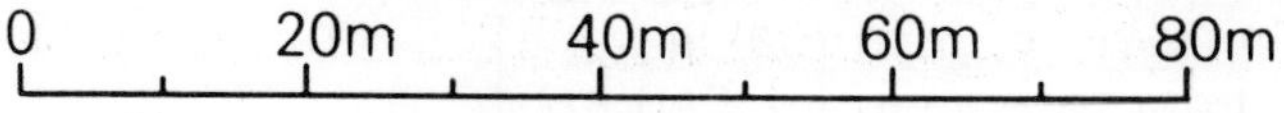

1 Use a ruler to measure. Complete chart A.

A

	Using a ruler	Real life
Main St.	16cm	160m
Cross St.		
Park Road		
Back Lane		
Moon Cres.		
Bent Row		

Use Chart B

2 a) Draw in the routes using coloured crayons.
b) Use a piece of string to measure the routes.
c) Complete Chart B.

B

Colour	From	To	Distance
Red	PS	N	100m
Blue	BG	Sch	
Yellow	10, Main St.	12, Cross St.	
Green	12, Back Lane	B	
Orange	⊕	LC	
Purple	7, Moon Cres.	PO	
Pink	F	 🦆	

Routes 3

MAP A   Scale 1:2500

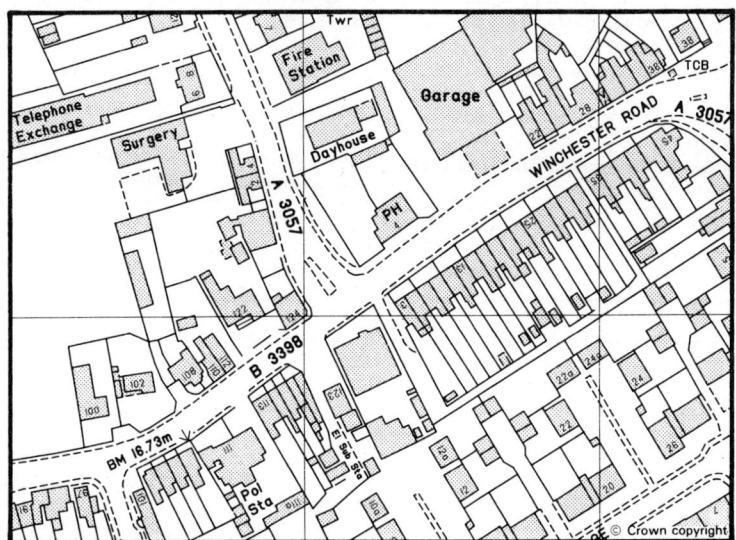

On Map A draw in the following routes:—

Colour	From	To
Red	28 Winchester Rd	Public House
Blue	Fire Station	36 Winchester Rd
Yellow	Surgery	Police Station
Green	Telephone exchange	Garage

On Map B draw these routes:—

Colour	From	To
Red	Offices	Zoological Gardens
Blue	Cemetery Lake	Hotel
Yellow	School	Garage
Green	Club	Public House

MAP B   Scale 1:10,000

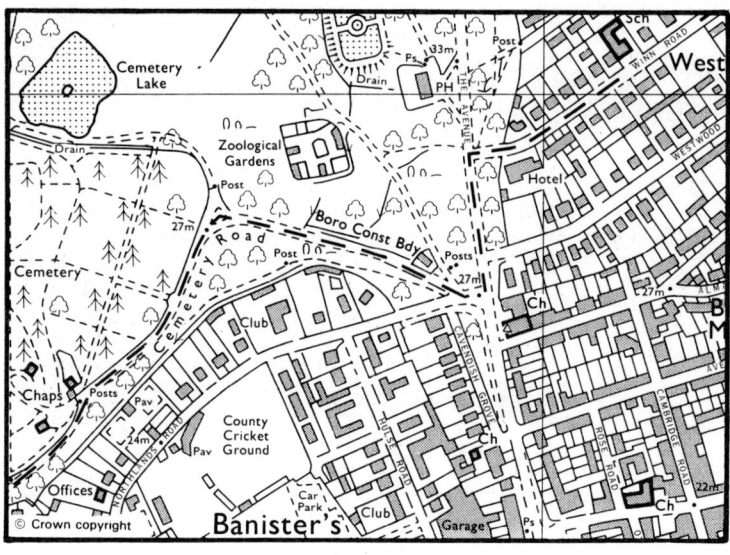

On Map C draw these routes:—

Colour	From	To
Red	Old Dad's House	Abbott House
Blue	Osbaldeston	P.O. at Mellor Brook
Yellow	Balshaw Fold Farm	Library
Green	Police Station	Dick Dadds

Different scales of map provide different information. When planning a journey we need to select the best map.

Use Maps A, B and C. Tick the map or maps you could use.

MAP C   Scale 1:25,000

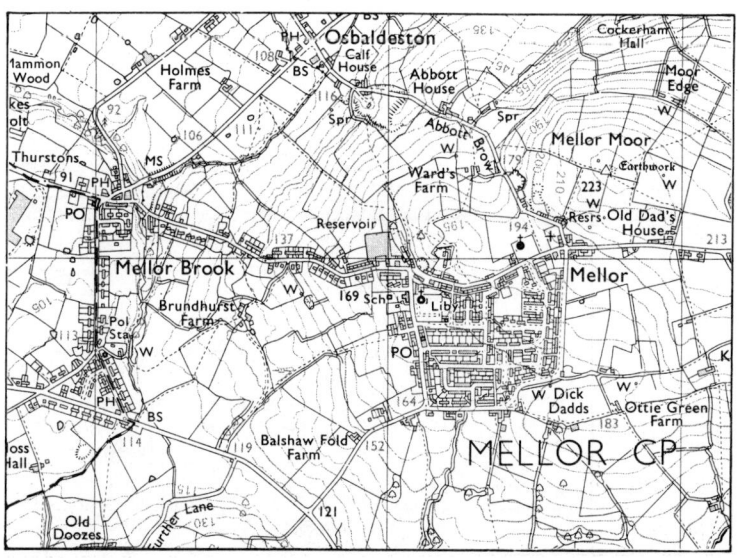

Activities	A 1:2500	B 1:10 000	C 1:25 000
Identify house numbers			
Travel between villages			
Read street names			
Identify church symbols			
Read contour lines			
Locate pavements			
Identify garages and outbuildings			

© Collins Educational: Harrisons/OS Resource Book ▶ You may photocopy this page for use in the classroom ◀

Grid References

BASIC IDEA
To understand how to read grid references and ultimately use 6 figure grid references.

	TARGETS FOR CHILDREN	
	TO KNOW	BE ABLE TO
STAGE 1	The term grid reference and why we use them.	Use simple 2 figure grid references. Letter/number in spaces.
STAGE 2	The difference between grid refs. Identifying spaces/whole squares/lines. Know term co-ordinate.	Use letter/figure, number/number 2 figure references. Grid references on lines and spaces. Plan own 2 figure co-ordinates.
STAGE 3	Know the terms 'Easting' and 'Northing'. Know that 4 figure co-ordinates refer to a whole square.	Be able to give co-ordinates to others using 'Easting, Northing'. Use 4 figure grid references. Use co-ordinates to describe a grid square on an OS map.
STAGE 4	To know and appreciate the need for accurate co-ordinate locations.	Use 6 figure grid references accurately on 1:50,000 OS map.

It is important to recognise that pupils may encounter grid references in areas other than geography. Such references occur in Maths work and in commercial games such as 'Battleships'.

Grid referencing is a crucial skill for all who are to feel confident in mapwork. By the end of the stages described here we expect pupils to use six-figure grid references.

Starting Points

A two-figure grid reference is best introduced on a letter/number basis. Children should learn always to start by running their finger along the horizontal axis — the Easting.

Using the Worksheets

Grid References 1 The Easting is identified first and then the Northing (vertical axis). At this level the children should be clear that the reference refers to the whole square. This is the case when the letters/numbers sit in the middle of squares and not on the lines.

Ref. B2 refers to the whole square

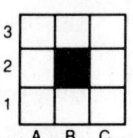

Grid References 2 continues with references which refer to whole squares but instead of letter/number we use number/number. Now the importance of using a standard format becomes apparent. Two numbers are meaningless unless there is a shared convention of Easting first then Northing. Pupils need to work co-operatively in pairs for this exercise. It is meant to be fun and ought to be enjoyed. A challenge worth presenting to the class is for them to devise similar games based on the same principle.

Grid References 3 can be seen as a transition point. The pupils no longer give references to whole squares based on mid-line letters/numbers. Instead the letters/numbers are *on* the line and the pupils note where the two lines intersect.

Ref. B, 1 refers to the point where the lines cross.

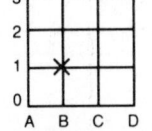

The activity is to join the grid reference points in order to draw a giraffe.

Children can extend this activity by designing their own grid animals, plotting co-ordinates and asking their partners to complete the sheets.

Grid References 4 completes the transition. The pupils are once again identifying the contents of a whole square (as they did in worksheets 1 and 2). The difference now is that the location of the appropriate square is based on the numerical co-ordinates in the *South West* corner of the square.

25,12 refers to the whole square

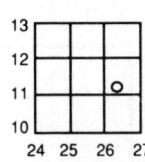

We are now working with 4 fig. grid references in order to locate whole squares. This has a limited application for pupils except as a step towards specific locations using 6 fig. grid references.

Grid References 4 requires the children to identify the squares using 4 figs. and to record the contents. The process is then reversed as they work from the contents to the grid references.

The linking teaching point between **Grid References 4 & 5** is the inadequacy of the 4 fig. ref. technique for the accurate location of an object which does not fill a whole square.

Thus if we say there is a ball in square (26,11) we are not sufficiently explicit about the exact location of the ball within the square.

This point can be developed for pupils by playing a game in pairs.

Each child has an identical blank grid (25 squares) and a set of symbols. Sitting opposite each other but separated by a temporary partition child A gives instructions to B as to the square in which the symbol should be placed — this is to mirror the sheet of child A. No instruction other than the 4 fig. grid ref. should be given. When the exercise is completed the two sheets are compared and sheet A will differ from sheet B in the detailed location of the symbol within the square.

This presents a problem which the pupils can be asked to try and resolve. The square should be sub-divided into 100 smaller squares allowing much more detailed references.

Working from the earlier identified difficulty, one square can be taken and enlarged, it can then be sub-divided into 100 smaller squares. The ball that could not earlier be clearly located now exists within a specific square.

The ball is now clearly at point (263,112)

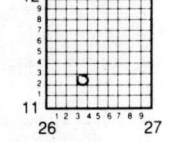

There is a need for a lengthy and detailed discussion about six-figure grid references. **Grid References 5** is not easy but seeks to assess the degree to which the concept has been understood. It requires a simultaneous knowledge of OS symbols, although a symbol sheet (legend) could be provided at the teacher's discretion.

WORKSHEET	SKILLS INVOLVED	SKILLS PRACTISED IN	
		BOOK 1	BOOK 2
1 The Invaders	Letter/number 2 figure grid references. Using spaces between lines	p. 11 p. 23 p. 26/27	p. 4/5
2 Rama and Sita	Number/number 2 figure grid references in spaces Working in pairs		
3 The Grid Giraffe	Letter/number 2 figure grid references on lines Plotting co-ordinates		
4 Ghosts and Ghouls	4 figure grid reference		
5 OS Conventional Signs	Accurate location of 6 figure grid references		p. 26/27

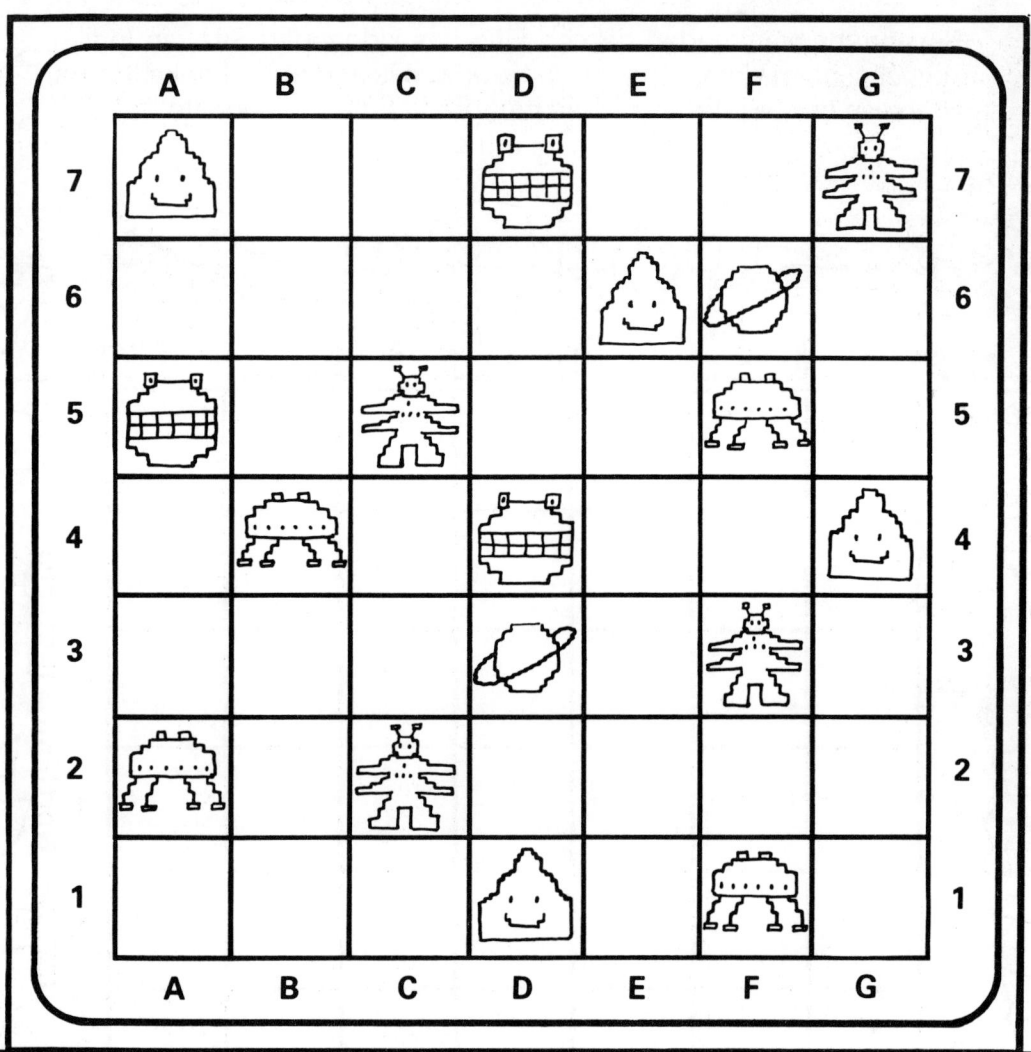

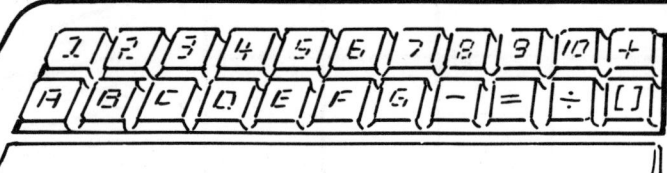

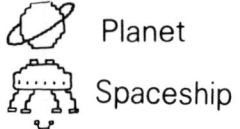

Grid References 1   The Invaders

Planet	Rocket
Spaceship	Munch machine
Alien	Jellyteens

You are being attacked by beings from outer space.

1 First you must locate them. Complete this location chart.

Grid Ref.	Picture	Description
A,2		Spaceship
C5		
G4		
D7		
B4		

2 Now you must contact all the invaders. Complete this contact chart.

Contact	Grid References
Spaceships	A2, B4, F1, F5
Aliens	
Munch machines	
Jellyteens	

3 You decide to send rockets to have a closer look.

Draw rockets in grid squares C3, D5, G3, B7, D2, A1, E4, F2.

4 The invaders return to their planets.

Give the grid references _____ _____

Grid References 2   Rama and Sita

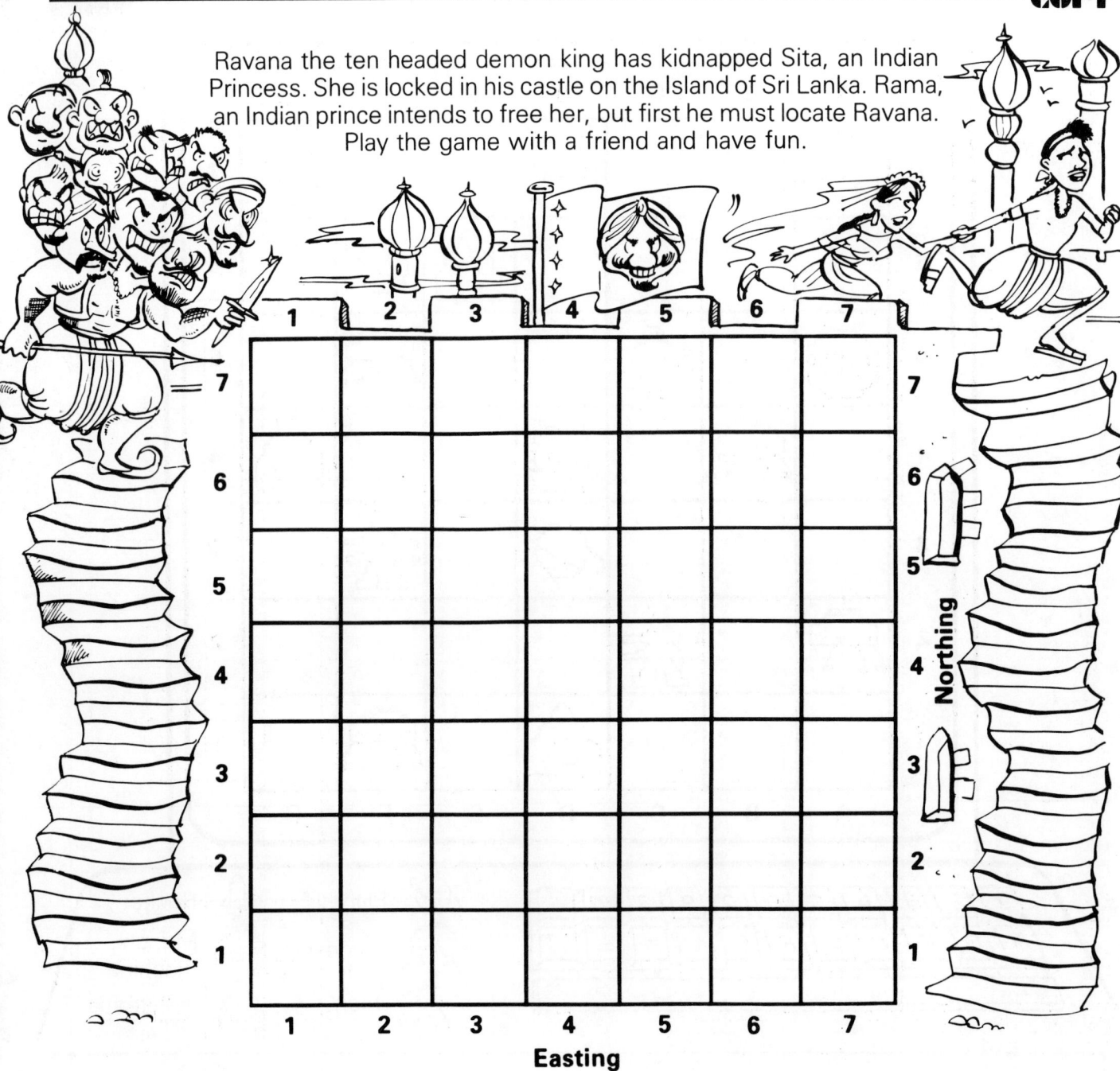

Ravana the ten headed demon king has kidnapped Sita, an Indian Princess. She is locked in his castle on the Island of Sri Lanka. Rama, an Indian prince intends to free her, but first he must locate Ravana. Play the game with a friend and have fun.

Northing (vertical axis, 1–7)
Easting (horizontal axis, 1–7)

How to play: 2 Players

1. Each player starts with a copy of this sheet.
2. Draw Ravana's 10 heads in different grid squares (don't let your partner see it).
3. Take turns. Give a grid ref. to your partner, if she has drawn a head in that square you have destroyed it and can have another turn.
4. The first one to locate the ten heads drawn by your partner is the winner and has freed Sita.

Write the grid references you choose below. This will make sure you don't ask for one twice.

© Collins Educational: Harrisons/OS Resource Book ▶ You may photocopy this page for use in the classroom ◀

Grid References 3   The Giraffe

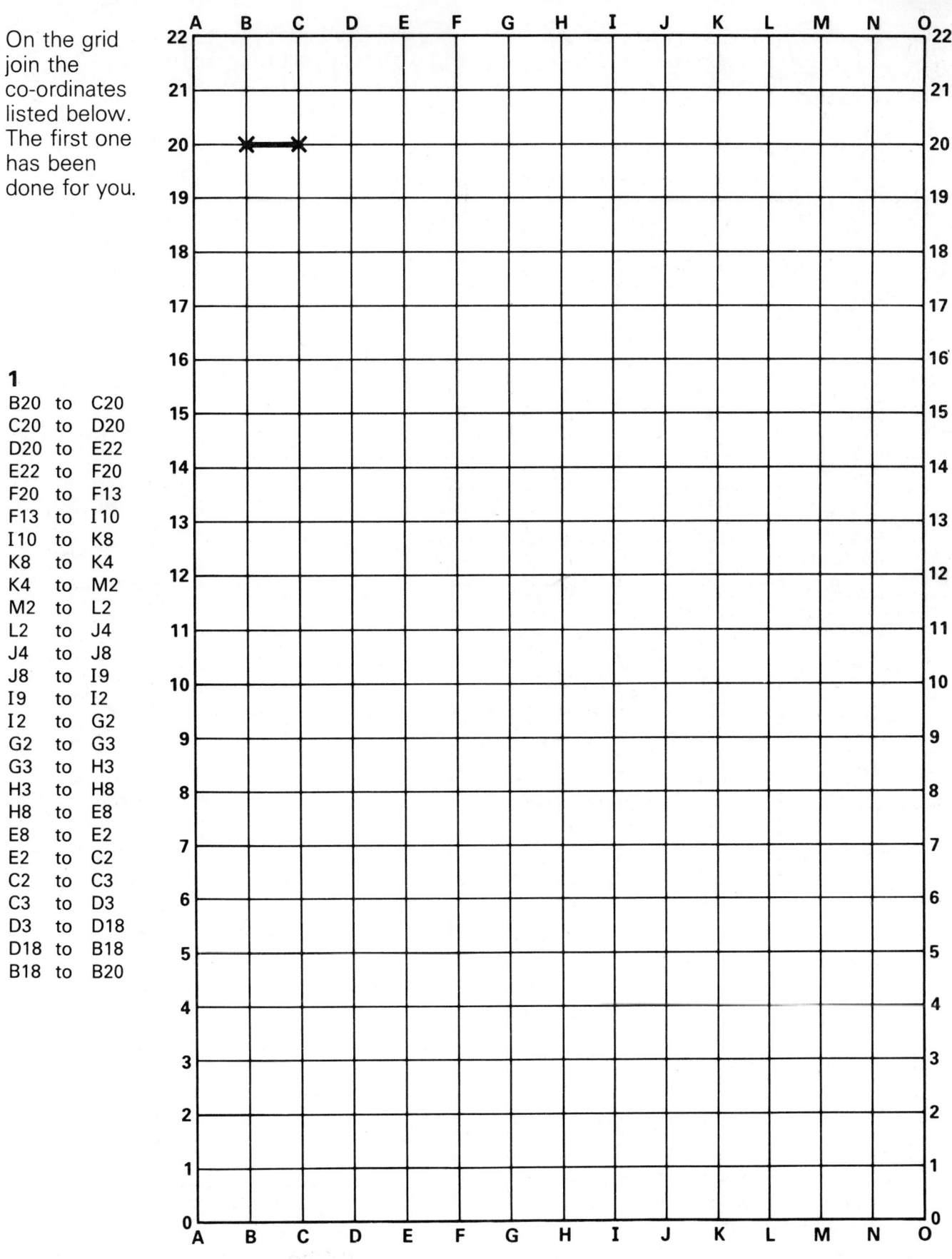

On the grid join the co-ordinates listed below. The first one has been done for you.

1

B20	to	C20
C20	to	D20
D20	to	E22
E22	to	F20
F20	to	F13
F13	to	I10
I10	to	K8
K8	to	K4
K4	to	M2
M2	to	L2
L2	to	J4
J4	to	J8
J8	to	I9
I9	to	I2
I2	to	G2
G2	to	G3
G3	to	H3
H3	to	H8
H8	to	E8
E8	to	E2
E2	to	C2
C2	to	C3
C3	to	D3
D3	to	D18
D18	to	B18
B18	to	B20

2 a) Using 1cm² paper draw a different grid animal.

b) Plot the co-ordinates.

c) Give the co-ordinates to a friend. Did they get it right?

Grid References 4

GHOSTS and GHOULS

Play the Ghosts and Ghouls Game.
Get them before they get YOU! You must locate them.

1 Complete the location charts.

a)
Grid reference	Description
18,40	Rat
19,42	
20,46	
16,44	
14,45	
15,46	

b)
Grid Reference	Description
17,46	Ghost with big feet
	Lady with no head
	Spells book
	Broomstick
	House
	Frogs

Grid References 5   Using 6 figure grid references

Use the Conventional signs on page 31 of 'Master Maps with OS'.

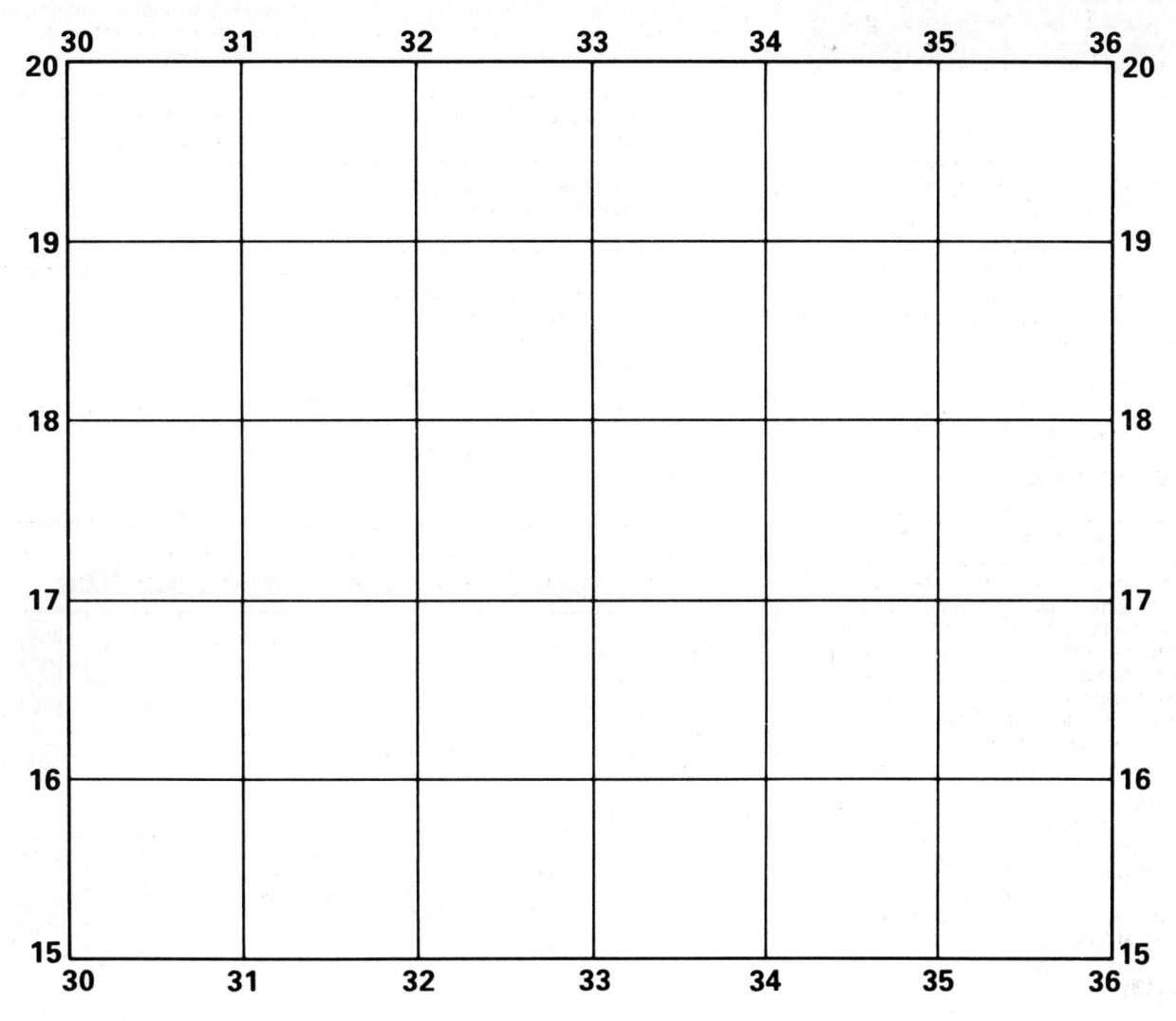

Legend

Follow the instructions to make a map.

1. A motorway runs due North starting at grid ref. 324,150.
2. Draw a motorway junction at grid ref. 324,173.
3. A main road runs East to West crossing the motorway junction.
4. A single track railway starts at grid ref. 300,164 and travels due East finishing at grid ref. 360,164.
5. There is a railway cutting from 344,164 to 350,164.
6. There is a railway embankment from 305,164 to 310,164.
7. A coniferous wood covers the whole of grid squares 340,190 and 350,190.
8. Public buildings lie on the North side of the road from 340,175 to 349,175.
9. A Public house is located at 355,175.
10. A freight line railway runs from a quarry at 352,158 to the railway station at 357,164. Draw the quarry and the line.
11. Draw a legend for your map.

Location

BASIC IDEAS
**Understand location.
Recognise the need to identify locations accurately.**

As with all constituent elements of mapping, location needs to be understood in relation to the closely associated areas of plan, grid reference and direction. Children are aware of basic locations — the position of furniture in the classroom, the site of a playground or a dangerous crossroads. Those who visit a large supermarket will be conversant with the fact that cereals come after vegetables and chocolate is always near the checkout. When supermarkets change the location of certain goods, in order to increase casual sales, children recognise the change as a difference in location.

Starting Points
Discussion about the location of everyday objects is useful. The teacher's desk is *near* the door, the maths table is *between* the bookshelf and the sink. Children can be asked about the location of features in their own home — the T.V. set, the telephone etc. As the focus widens, the location of public facilities can be addressed — where is the nearest telephone booth located? What is the location of the postbox, newsagent, chip shop etc.

Location is always relative. We indicate the location of the postbox in relation to other features we know from experience and from using maps. This involves the recognition of those features and the use of appropriate locational language.

Display
When using large scale local maps in order to stress location work it is advisable to make the map the centrepiece of a display.

Photographs or children's drawings of the locality can then be mounted around the map. The mapping ribbon can connect the photo to the actual location.

Fieldwork
Photographs taken by the teacher, in advance, can be given to the pupils as they move out into the local environment. Children working in pairs can identify the location of places/objects in the photos. They can mark them on their fieldwork map extract.

		TARGETS FOR CHILDREN	
		TO KNOW	BE ABLE TO DO
STAGE 1		Features of the local area and recognise on a large scale map. Locational language of the immediate environment e.g. street, road, avenue, roundabout, traffic lights, post box, village, town centre, park etc.	Read a plan of a desk top and recognise location of artefacts. Read a plan of a classroom and recognise locations — library etc. Read a plan of the school to locate classrooms etc.
STAGE 2		Know and use the terms location, located. Locational language:— T. Junction, crossroads, Town, City, housing, housing estate, inland/coastland etc.	Able to recognise and describe a location using a large scale (1:1250) OS map.
STAGE 3		Know and use terms Easting, Northing. Locational language:— County, Country, Central business district, industrial estate, leisure, cul de sac, square, inner city, populated.	From a written description find a location on a 1:25,000 OS map.
STAGE 4		Know and use locational language with ease. Easting, Northing, suburbs, urban/rural, dense/sparse. Road features.	Using locational language be able to describe accurately an area on an OS 1:50,000.

Street Furniture in our Locality

An extension activity for pupils who are displaying expertise and understanding is for the teacher to take a series of photos from various unusual angles and positions. The task for the children is to identify the location of the object in the photo *and* to mark on their map the points *from which* the photos were taken.

Smaller Scale Maps
When considering location in a wider context it is useful to use a 1:10,000 or 1:25,000 scale in order to discuss the location of well known local features — a sports ground, leisure centre, church, hypermarket, etc. The 1:50,000 is more usefully focussed on the location of settlements — north of the river, between A and B, where the A123 and the B456 meet etc.

Using the Worksheets

Location 1 — provides a classroom plan which will require the use of a key in addition to locational skills. The tasks develop from naming a location to matching locations to activities. This should be reinforced by the use of a similar plan of the children's own classroom or school, supported by appropriate questions.

Location 2 — moves into the local environment and should also be followed by the use of a large scale local OS map. Again there is a stress on choice of location for specific purposes. The pupil must consider options in order to solve the problem.

Location 3 — uses an urban area and extends the opportunity for pupils to address questions of location through the application of judgement. They must not only identify the best locations but must state their reasons for the choice. Once again a map of the local area can throw up similar questions and *actual* locations can be judged against *preferred* pupil locations.

			SKILLS PRACTISED IN	
1	Classroom Locations	Matching location to activity	p. 2	p. 10
2	Park Locations	Identifying location Selecting suitable locations	p. 4 p. 10, 11, 12, 13	p. 7, 22/23 p. 28, 29
3	Town Planner	Problem solving Selecting locations Co-operating in a group	p. 17, 18	p. 18/19 p. 24/25

Location 1   Classroom Locations

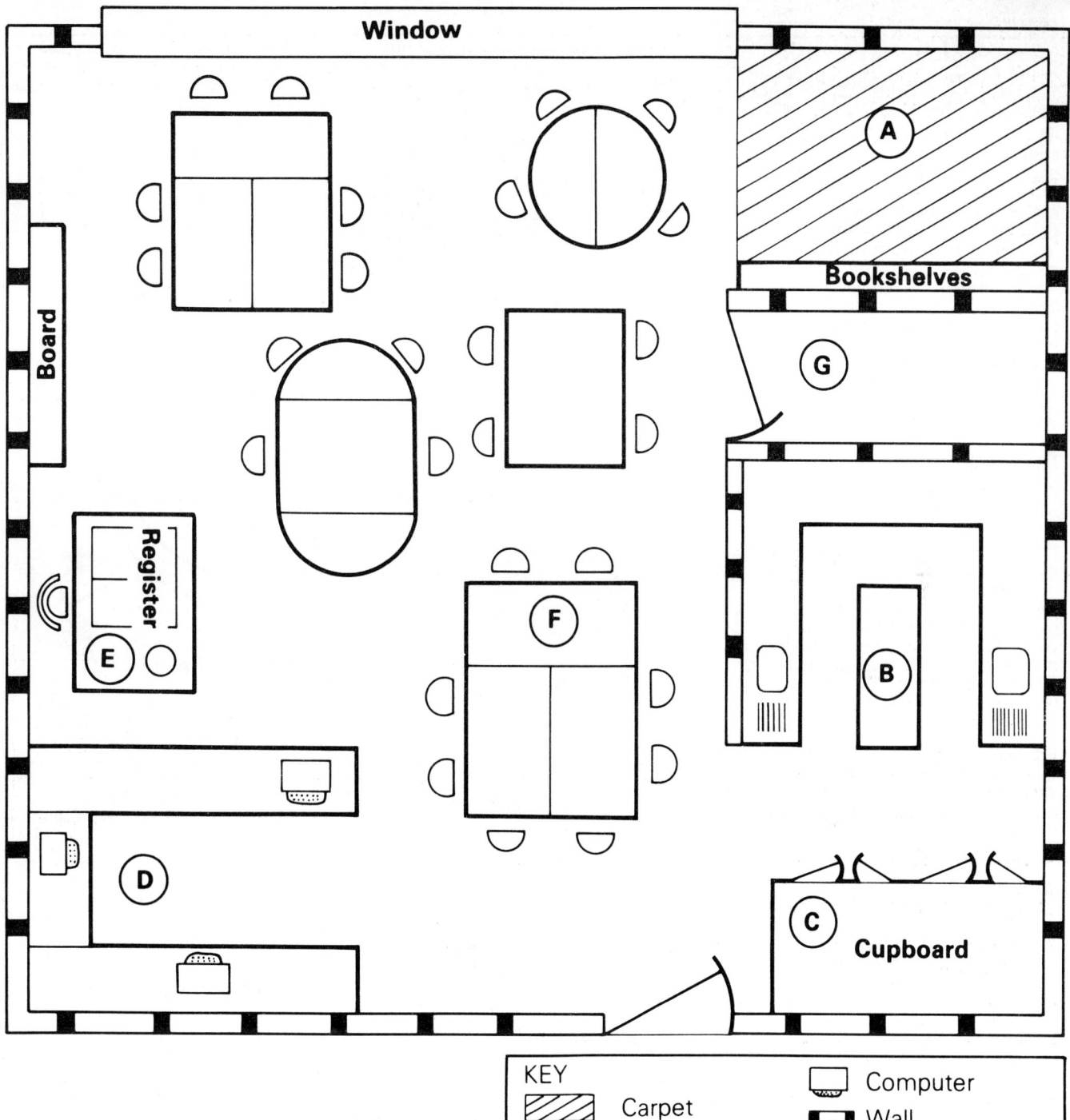

Look at the locations A to G.

1 Match the letters to the actual locations.

Area	Letter
Art and Craft	B
Computers	
Child's place	
Stock room	
Teacher's desk	
Maths cupboard	
Reading corner	

KEY
- Carpet
- Sink
- Computer
- Wall
- Door

2 Which location would be most suitable for the following activities?

Location	Activity
B	Paint a picture
	Choose a book
	Use a computer
	Store spare paper
	Get a pair of scales
	Wash a paint brush

© Collins Educational: Harrisons/OS Resource Book ▶ You may photocopy this page for use in the classroom ◀

Location 2   Park Locations

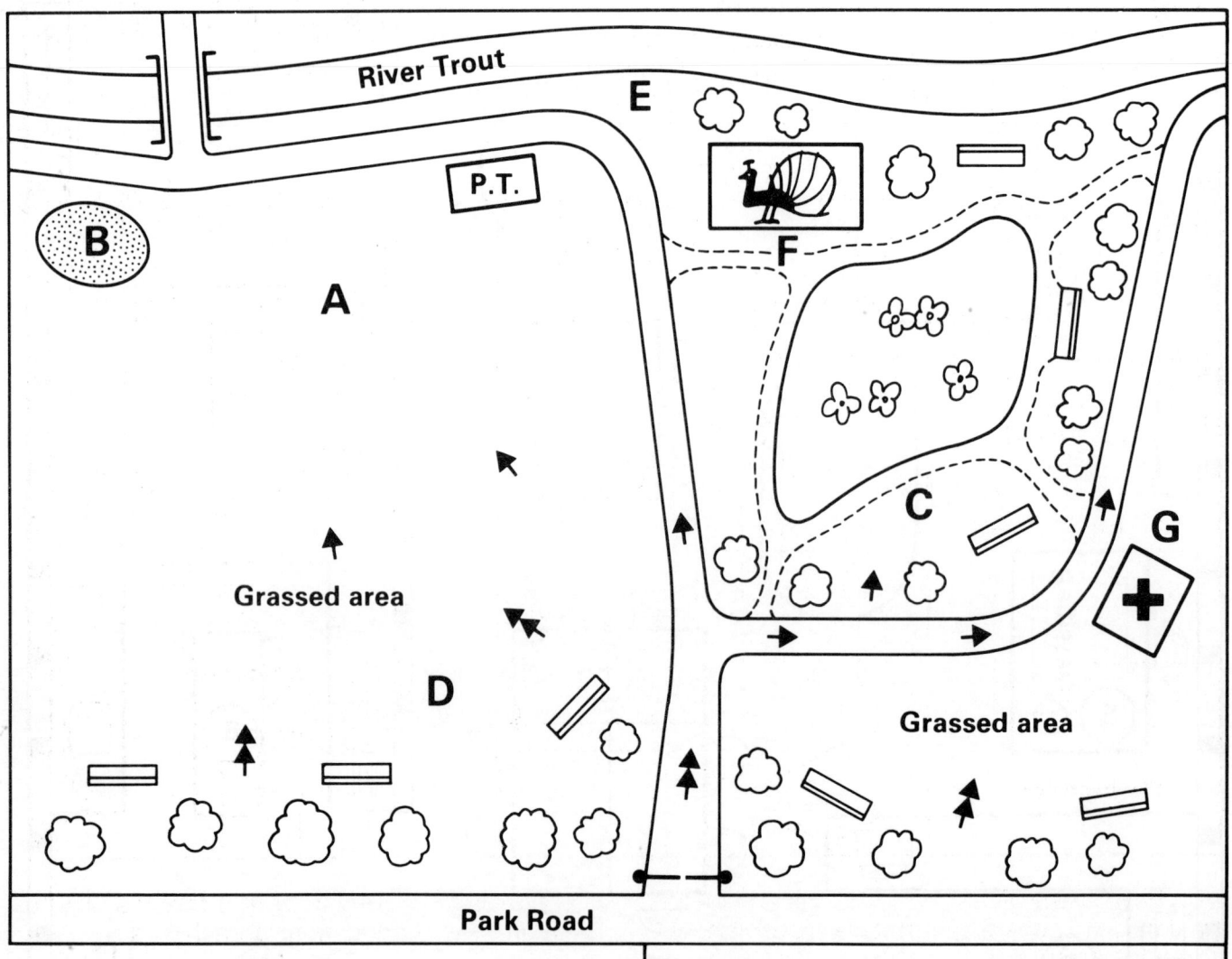

Look at locations A to G.

1 Which location would be the best for the following activities?

Location	Activity
E	Catch fish
	Look at the peacocks
	Build a sandcastle
	Play rolling downhill on the grass
	Eat a picnic beside the pond
	Play football
	Bandage a cut leg

2 Complete the chart.

Land surface	Location
Flat	
Sloping	
Steep	

KEY

- Peacock House
- First Aid
- Lily pond
- Sandpit
- P.T. Public toilets
- Park gates
- Park bench
- Footpath
- ➤ Sloping ground
- ➤➤ Steep ground

3 Design symbols for

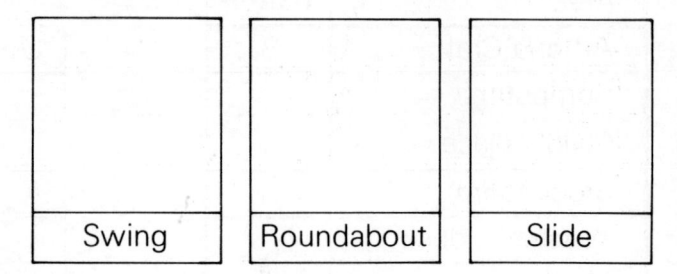

Swing	Roundabout	Slide

4 Draw them on the plan in the most suitable location.

Location 3   Town Planner

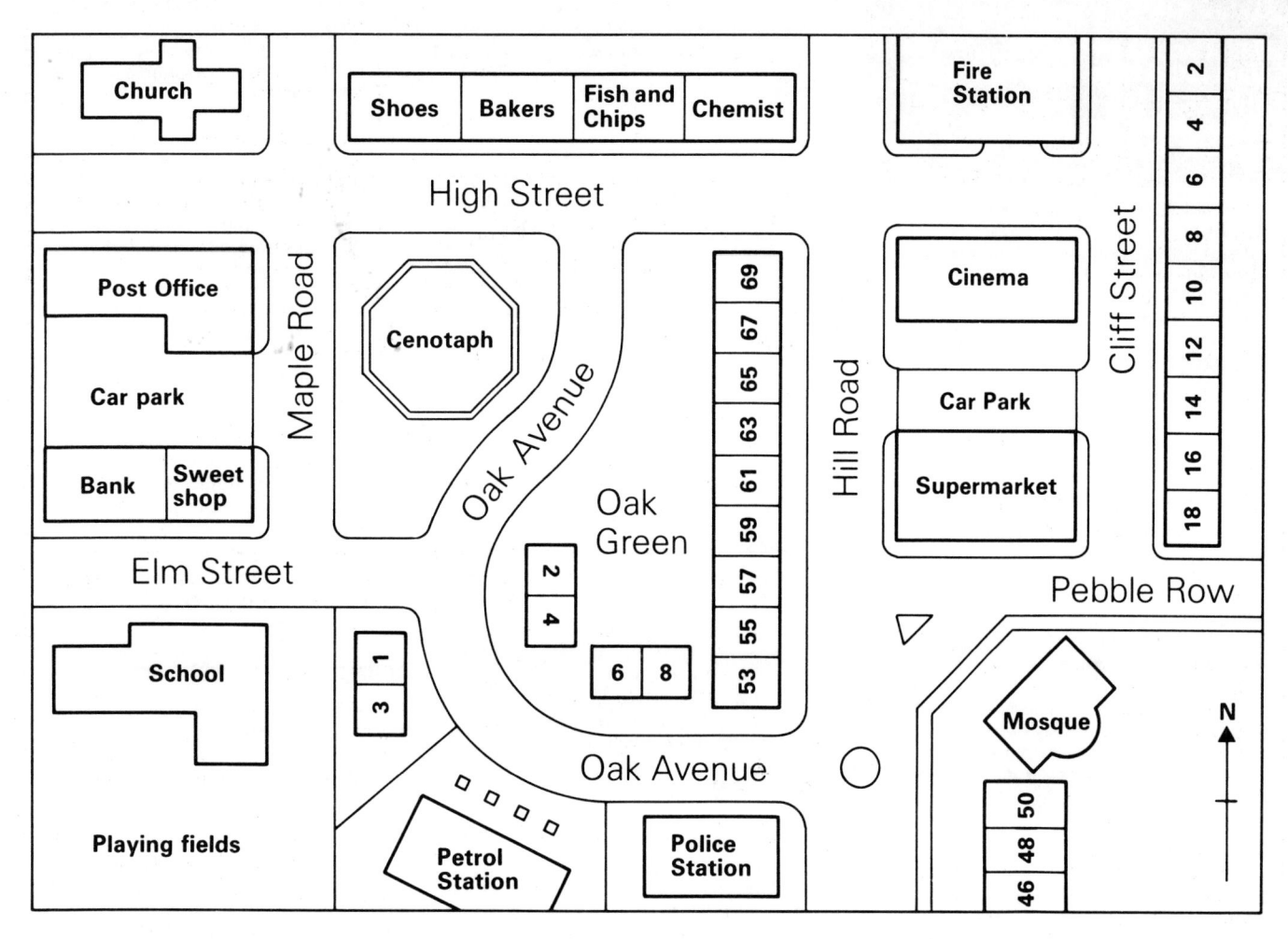

You have been given the job of planning the best place to put street furniture. You will have to think carefully about busy places, dangerous places etc. and give good reasons for your decisions.

1 Complete the chart.

2 Compare your chart with a friend's. Try to agree on the location of each.

3 In a group discuss the differences in opinions. Try to agree on the best reasons for the location of each.

Street Furniture	Location	Reason
Pelican crossing	High St. Church to P.O.	On Sundays people will park behind the P.O. and go to church
Pelican crossing		
Traffic lights		
Traffic lights		
Litter bin		
Litter bin		
Public bench		
Public bench		
Public bench		
Post box		
Post box		
Telephone box		

© Collins Educational: Harrisons/OS Resource Book ▶ You may photocopy this page for use in the classroom ◀

Height

BASIC IDEAS

Relief and the need for it.
Understand and depict height on maps.
Understand the purpose of contour lines.

| | TARGETS FOR CHILDREN ||
	TO KNOW	BE ABLE TO DO
STAGE 1	Height vocabulary, big/bigger/biggest, as big as, twice the size of, half the height of, etc.	Estimate proportional height using height vocabulary. Depict height in drawings. Modelling to a reasonable representation. Observe carefully the landscape, discuss heights of buildings etc.
STAGE 2	Know and use height vocabulary with ease, deep/depth, storey, floor, highland/lowland, steep/gentle. Know and use the term 'relief'.	Observe height differences and be able to draw a sketch map indicating them using colour shading and key. Recognise the difference between relief map and plan.
STAGE 3	Know geographical terms such as, mountain, hill, ridge, valleys, river, valley, water flow, estuary, plain etc.	Able to use layer colouring as a form of relief. Introduction to contour lines through comparison with layer colouring.
STAGE 4	To know and use precise geographical language in relation to OS maps, contour, spot height, summit etc.	Draw in the contour lines on a map as an accurate form of relief. Be able to recognise height by reading the contour lines on an OS 1:50,000.

Many adults have difficulty interpreting height on a map and younger children should not be pushed too early into interpreting maps for height. The conceptual level is relatively sophisticated.

Starting Points

Plan view tells us nothing about height. Until this is understood the need for a technique for depicting height will not be appreciated.

Simple Layer Colouring

This is the simplest way to depict height. It is advisable to start with no more than 3 levels. The school's grounds are often appropriate. An area where steps, bins, fences are found is ideal. A simple plan of the site should be used and the ground is depicted as 0m. Objects on the site are then measured by pupils working in groups of 2/3. An appropriate scale would be 0-1m yellow, 1-2m red, 2+m blue. Pupils could of course choose their own scale and colour key. The map will then depict height through colour.

Aerial photographs can also be used to reinforce this point. It is advisable to begin with an aerial view of your own locality and to focus on buildings. Once the children have talked about the aerial view they should observe and record some of the buildings in the area from ground level.

Buildings can be classified by storey. Agreement should then be arrived at to colour code the different storeys (e.g. buildings of 1 storey — green, 2/3 blue, 4/6 red, 7/10 yellow etc.). Storey is an arbitrary measure and it is worth considering the use of a clinometer in order to establish the actual height of buildings. The colour coding can then be applied to a range (0-5 green etc.). Using a large scale local map colour can be added so that the approximate height of buildings is shown. (Remember the building height will be from the ground, this level of work ignores the height of the land itself, to do otherwise is to complicate matters beyond a child's comprehension.)

Wall maps and atlases which use simple colour layering for height of land should be in use at the same time. This will reinforce the child's understanding of the purpose and uses of the technique and the need to recognise that height is an important feature which needs to be mapped.

These kinds of activity should be supplemented by work in related areas. Craft work should concern itself with height in design, artwork ought to include elements of relief in drawing, painting and collage work.

Modelling

Three-dimensional modelling using plasticine/clay/papier maché etc. can be useful in recreating an observed landscape.
A group of children could take the 'Buried Treasure' spread from 'Master Maps' pp. 28/9 and model their own imaginary island. This would be landscaped and painted and would have a corresponding plan drawn for it. The pupils could provide clues about the location of treasure and challenge others in the class to find it.

Introducing Contours

Mapping real environments is crucial to understanding contours. This is a consideration to be borne in mind when schools plan visits and is another reason why a school policy is preferable to individual autonomy. We should aim to give pupils an introduction to different landscapes, townscapes and communities during their time in school.

The actual introduction of contour lines flows naturally from colour layering. In effect the lines remain but the colour is deleted. It is therefore important to stress the need for a clear black felt tip line to be drawn between colours on a colour layered map.

'Discover Maps' does not attempt to deal with height. It would be appropriate therefore to concentrate on contour work when the children are ready for 'Master Maps'.

Using the Worksheets

It is important to see the worksheets as exemplars. There is a need for a great deal of consolidation work between the stages covered by the worksheets.

Height 1 — This provides basic practice in colour relief layering. The jelly is divided by height and colour coded. The data is given in this instance but pupils can be encouraged to draw similar objects and choose their own scales and colour codes. The words 'contour lines' should be used as often as possible so as to become part of the child's vocabulary.

Height 2 — There is no side view on this occasion, simply a plan view with spot heights marked but not joined. The intention here is to get across the notion that contour lines join points of equal height.

Height 3 — The third step is to start from the contours and attempt to visualise the landscape they describe. This is, in effect, what we do with contours. We are provided with information on a 2-dimensional plane and we convert that information into a mental image of a 3-dimensional world. The pupils must choose the correct picture view which corresponds with the contour plan. Pupils can extend this by drawing their own contoured plans with views and inviting others to match them correctly.

'Master Maps' pp. 8/9 introduces contours by using an illustration of a slide with steep and gentle sides. The same concept can be explored with a piece of stiff card or strawboard. By folding the card at different points we can change the steepness of the two sides and mark vertical heights along the sides which are then joined to form contours. This demonstrates the rule that the closer together contour lines occur the steeper the slope.

		SKILLS PRACTISED IN	
1 Jelly	Colour relief		
2 Counting Contours	Drawing in contours Identifying heights		p. 8/9
3 Interpreting Contours	Plan view. Selecting correct side view.		p. 26/27

Height 1   Jelly on a dish

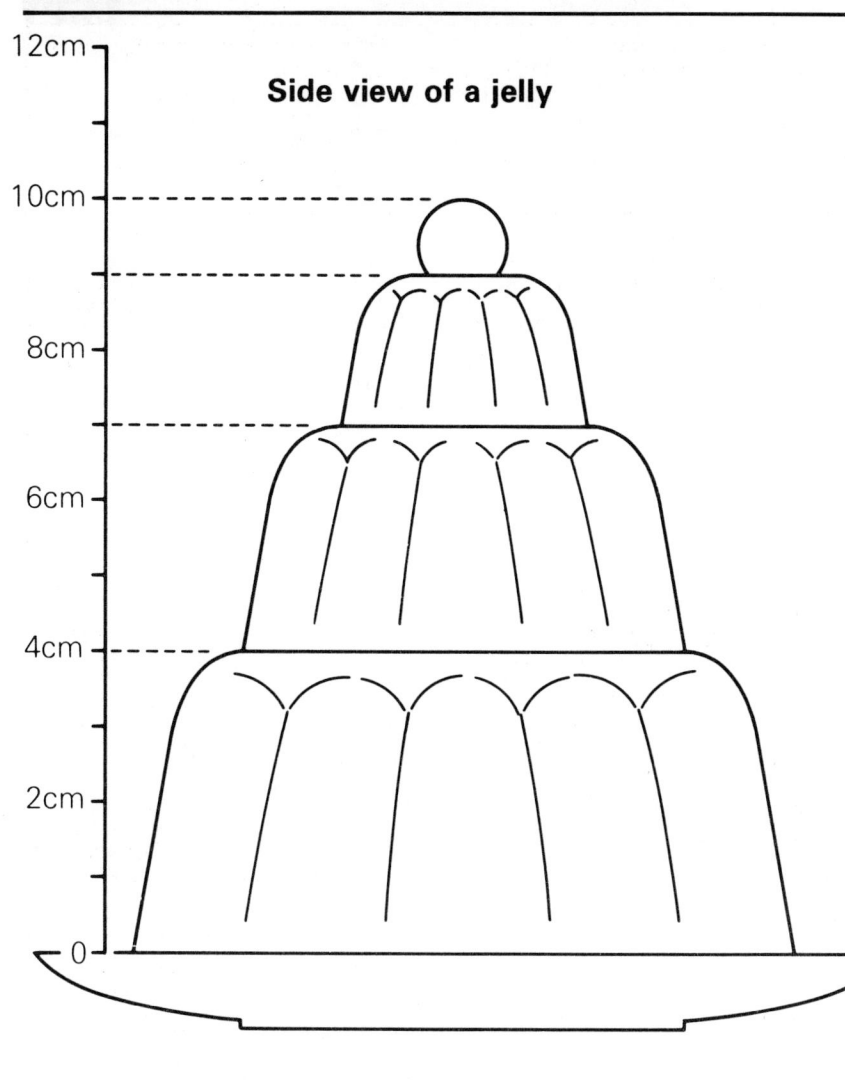

Side view of a jelly

(Scale: 0 to 12cm marked in 2cm intervals, with dashed lines at 4cm, 7cm, 9cm and 10cm)

Choose the best colour for each layer.

1 Colour the jelly.
   0-4cm is lime
   4-7cm is banana
   7-9cm is blackcurrant
   9-10cm is a cherry

2 Draw a colour key.

Colour key	
Height	Colour
0-4cm	

Plan view of the jelly

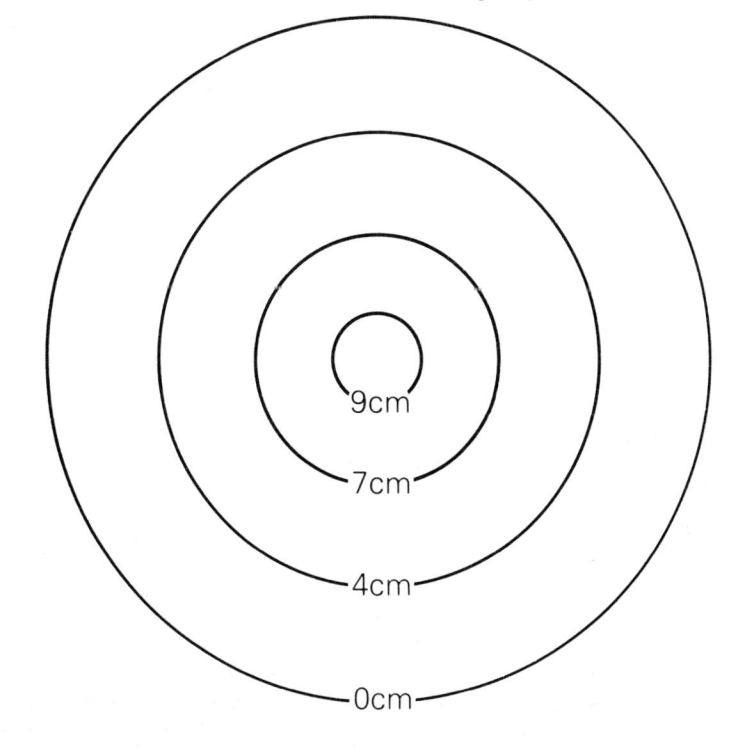

(Concentric circles labelled 9cm, 7cm, 4cm, 0cm)

3 Now look at the plan view of the jelly.
Use the same colour key to colour the plan of the jelly.

You have now shown height on the plan using different colours. We call this *colour relief*.

The lines where the colours meet are called *contour lines*.

Height 2 — Counting contours

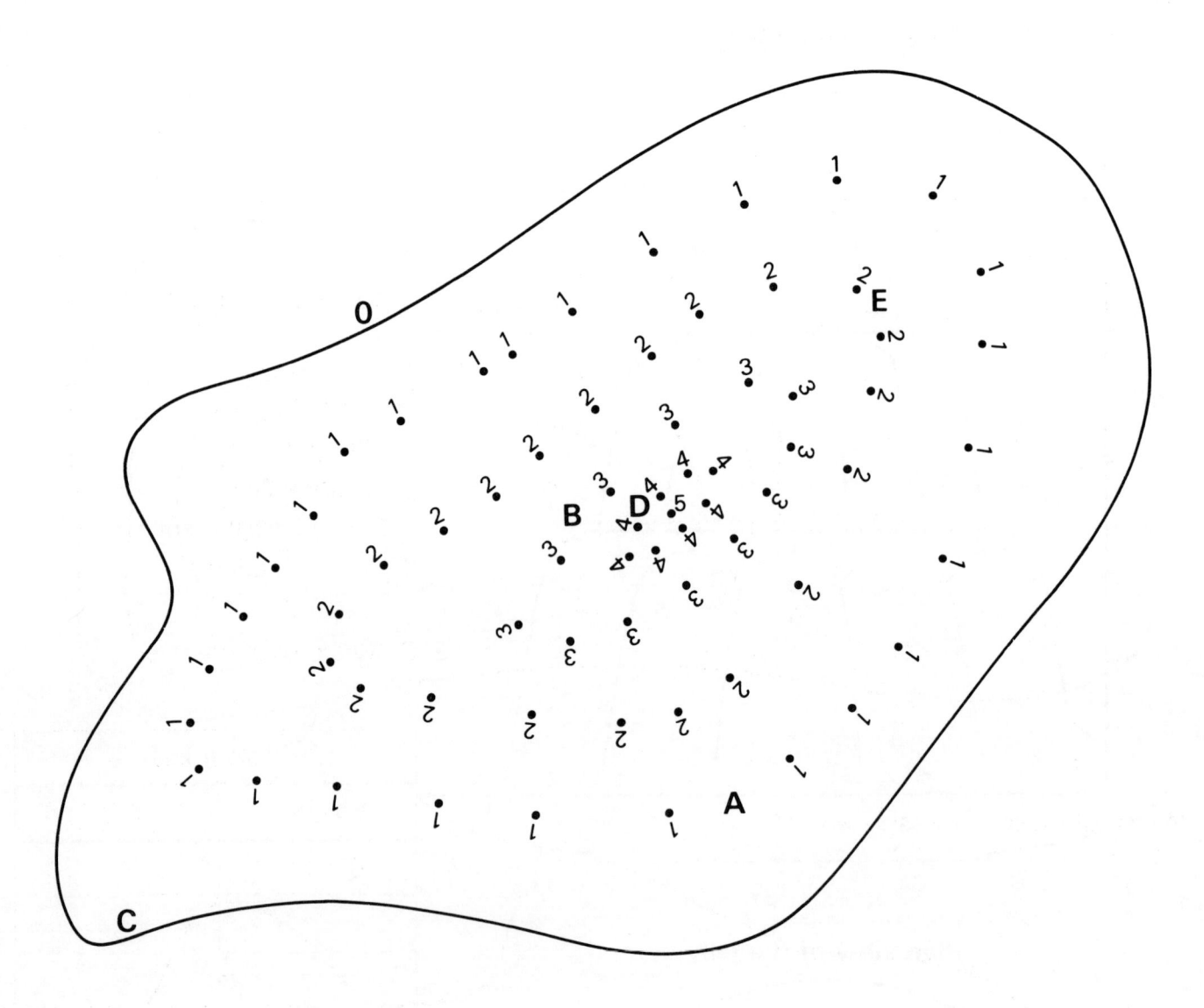

1. **Join up all the points of the same number.**
   You have now joined points of equal height and drawn *contour lines*.

2. **Colour the different levels.**
   Choose your own colours and complete the key.

Height	Colour
0-1	
1-2	
2-3	
3-4	
4-5	

3. **Look at the letters A to E. Give the height of each letter.**

A	
B	
C	
D	
E	

4. **Rearrange the letters putting the highest first.**

_ _ _ _ _

Height 3 Interpreting contours

Colour land between 50 - 100 Green   200 - 250 Red
             100 - 150 Blue   250 - 300 Purple
             150 - 200 Yellow Over 300 Orange

Plan view

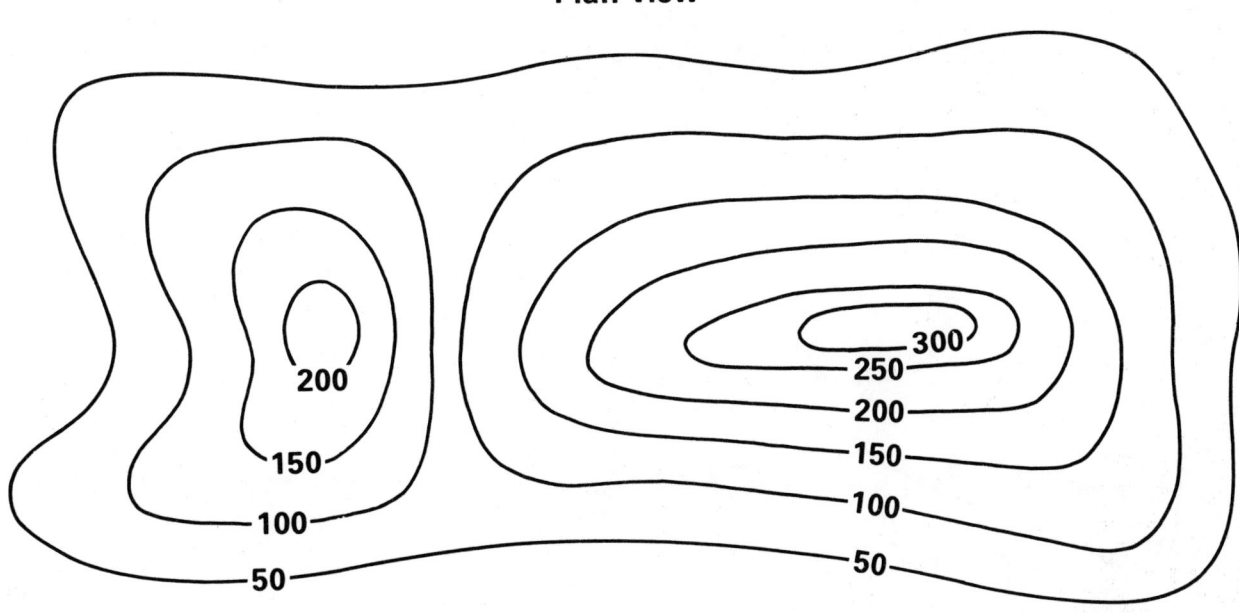

Which of these is the **side view?**

1

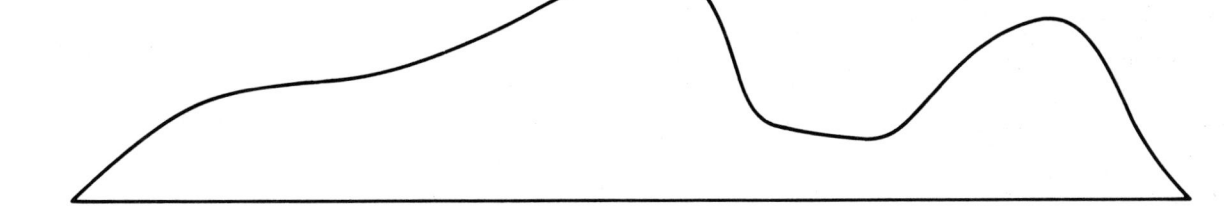

2

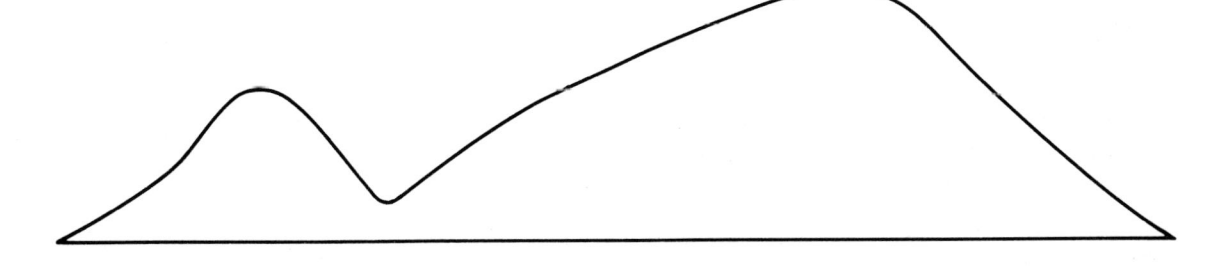

3

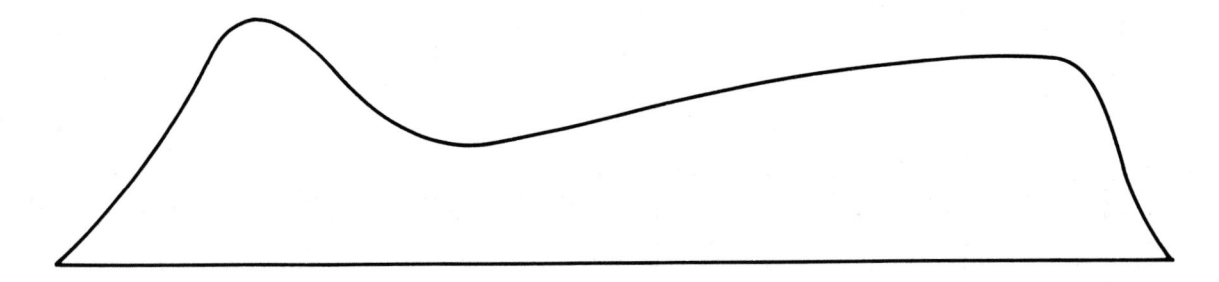

Using Photographs With Maps

Aerial Photography

Plan view is the view from above. It follows that if children are to understand fully what a map has to offer they need to see it in relation to a 'real' view from above.

In the early stages this is best introduced by photos of everyday objects taken from above. A desk top, milk bottle, cup, computer etc. can be photographed by the teacher and plans drawn. The photo, plan and object must then be matched by the pupils. Children can be encouraged to take their own photos from above and ask friends to identify them.

Access to a high rise building (office block/church etc.) is an obvious boon. If the facility can accommodate a group take 1:10,000 maps with you and view the area from above. Even without maps the activity is valuable. While 'on high' photograph the area and use the resulting photographs back in the classroom alongside maps. If you use a telephoto lens you may be better with a 1:1250/1:2500 map for small-area follow-up work.

Sources

There are a number of sources for true aerial photographs. The OS has a wide coverage in black and white. Local libraries and Records offices often contain a selection. Local newspapers have a variety and their archives may stretch back many years. This is particularly useful for examining changes over time. *Aerofilms* have a superb colour collection on transparencies for most of the country. They will send you contact prints in black and white for you to decide which is the best photo for your needs.

It is desirable to obtain an aerial photograph of the area in which the school is situated and where the pupils live. You may need to increase/reduce the relative sizes of map/photo in order to match them on scale. Most modern photocopiers have this facility. (Check that your school/l.e.a. has a licensing agreement with the OS for photocopying map extracts for use inside the institution.)

Pupils can work in pairs and identify features found on both the map and photographs. They are highly motivated when identifying their own home street/school etc. It is best to allow a period for open examination and discussion when no clear task is set. This discussion will be valuable in itself.

The class can then be asked to list what can be seen only on the map, only on the photo and on both. This will help in the understanding of what map makers include and what is excluded from maps.

You are allowed to photocopy pages 51 and 52; they are intended to reinforce the work encountered on pp 4 and 5 of 'Master Maps'. The area chosen is quite different to that in 'Master Maps' and pupils may find it interesting to compare the two. When using maps and photos of your local area it is important to select appropriate categories of land use reflected in the locality.

Children can sketch or photograph features from the local area (the front of their own home, the mosque, post office etc.) and display these along with aerial photo and map — linking their artwork to the views from above.

When sufficient practice has been provided in the local area it is important to provide pupils with aerial photographs of alternative locations. It is desirable for children to encounter rural, urban, coastal and highland aerial photographs during their time in school. The appropriate maps should be used with the photographs. Ideally a visit to the location will make the whole experience more meaningful.

Photographs of Distant Environments

Where members of the class are fortunate enough to enjoy a range of holidays it is sensible to ask them to return with a local map of the destination, a series of photographs taken on holiday and commercial postcards of the area. A description of aspects of the holiday can then be supported by mapwork, photo interpretation and a comparison between the 'reality' of the visit and the postcards which present a view which may be 'economical with the truth'.

Older pupils should be introduced to photo-packs and maps of distant U.K. and world environments. The personal network system is often the best way of obtaining the maps you want — a relative in Australia, a business friend in Nigeria, a colleague on VSO in Papua New Guinea etc.

A map of the UK/Europe/World can be the centrepiece of a display which uses photos for a comparison of different environments. Mapping pins and ribbon can lead from the map to a large display which features an environment with which the pupils are familiar and an alternative environment with which they are likely to be unfamiliar. Discussion, interpretation and the use of photographic evidence for identifying similarity and difference will follow. Discussion should include the landscape, evidence of economic activity, the people (dress, culture, ages, gender), the homes (styles, building materials, size), vegetation and climate. As ever it is important to select photographs of other locations which do not distort the real world. Britain is not full of beefeaters or wenches serving ale. France is not populated by onion sellers and the population of India does not spend its time alternating between begging and riding elephants.

Apart from taking your own photos for a display of your local area it is useful to contact local businesses, advertising agencies, councils, estate agents, building developers, development agencies, tourist offices etc. all of whom need photos from time to time and many of whom will be willing to donate their unused/unwanted stock to local schools.

Using Aerial Photos with Maps 1

1 Look at the aerial photograph.
What can you see? Tick the correct box.

LAND USE	YES	NO	CAN'T TELL
Transport			
Farming			
Leisure			
Housing			
Shipping			
Industrial			
Shopping			

2 Look at the map.
What can you see? Tick the correct box.

	YES	NO
Motorway		
Bus station		
Canal		
River		
Railway		
Airport		
Railway station		

© Collins Educational: Harrisons/OS Resource Book ▶ You may photocopy this page for use in the classroom ◀

Using Aerial Photos with Maps 2

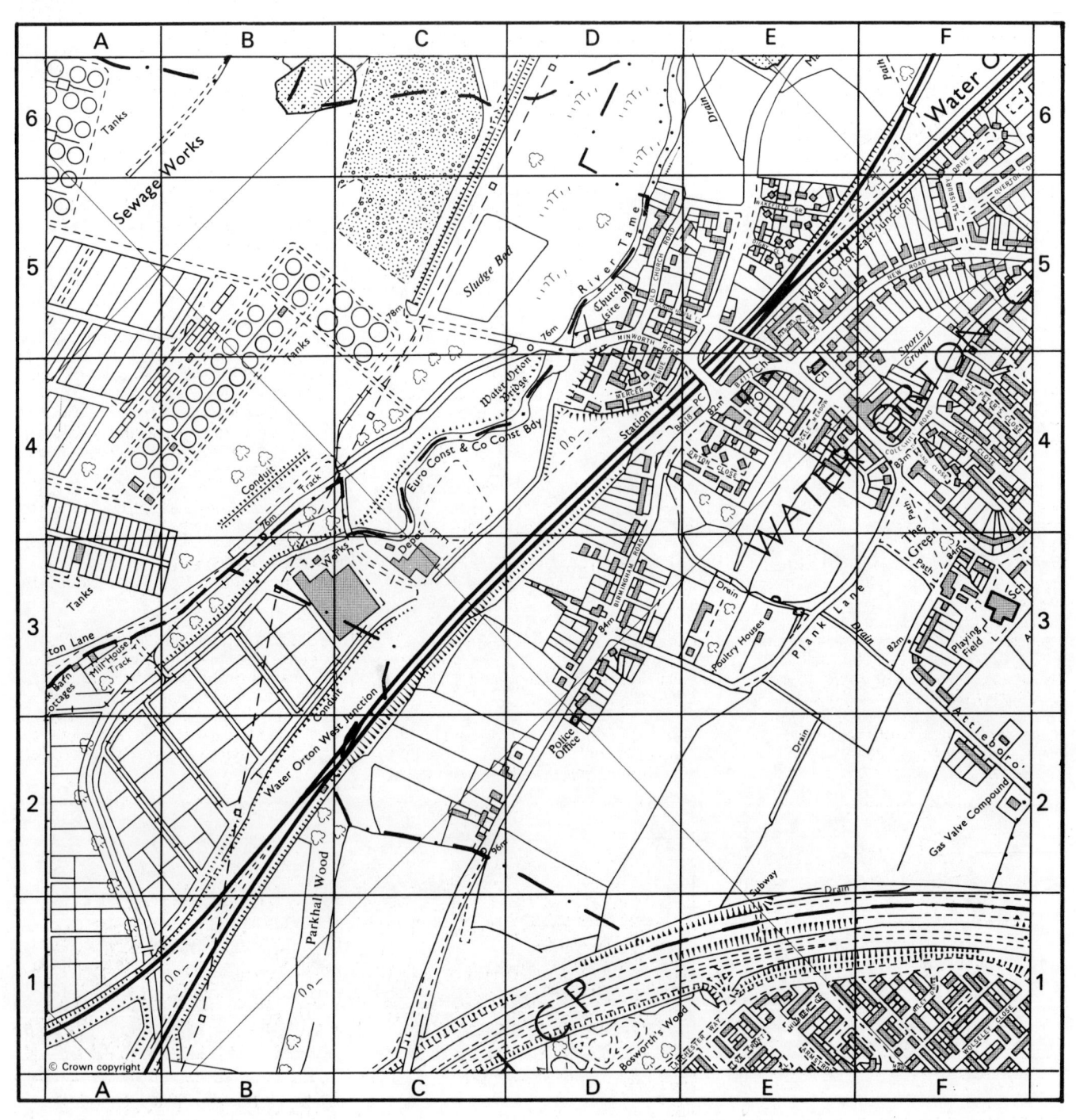

3 Look at the photograph and map.
Say which from the list can be seen only on the map/on the photo/on both.

	Photo	Map	Both
School			
Sewage works			
Traffic			
Road names			
Motorway			
Sewage tank arms			
Houses			
Subway			

4 Say how the land is mainly used in these grid squares.
F1, A6, B3, F6, D2, E2, C1, F4

LAND USE			
Housing	Agriculture	Transport	Industry
F1			

5 List the grid squares through which

a) The river runs _____

b) The motorway runs _____

Fieldwork and Mapping

It is important to remember that the mapping aspect of fieldwork is part of a two-way process. The site to be visited can be used as a vehicle for mapwork and in particular for the development of specific skills which a group of pupils are ready to learn and put into practice. Viewed in this way you would first identify the skills you wished to develop and you would then select a site to visit which provided opportunities to use those skills.

The alternative procedure is to choose a site for other reasons and to enhance the level and quality of the pupils' understanding of the site by aspects of mapwork. In this instance the reasons for site-selection may not include its mapwork potential but nevertheless you would seek to exploit an opportunity for mapping to take place.

Two examples taken from our own practice may be helpful in illustrating the point. A group of eleven year olds were in North Wales for a week's fieldwork. One aim of the week was to develop a sense of chronology by visiting a series of historical sites. Our visit to a Romano-British village was principally intended to serve this concept-building aim, but we took the opportunity to investigate the site in a number of ways. One such way was to map the site using compasses, trundle wheels and tape measures. A variety of mapping skills were used but they fulfilled a supplementary purpose.

On a separate occasion we wanted to concentrate on a basic understanding of height and contours. We therefore took our group of nine year olds to a hill which had one steep side and another side which sloped gently. The activities we pursued and the maps we took with us were focussed entirely on the objective of giving pupils practical experience of slopes. The site was chosen for its mapwork potential and for no other reason.

Fieldwork is difficult for some schools for a variety of reasons. Where this is the case it would be unrealistic to set aside many visits in order to practise specific map skills. As with much of what we do in schools there will probably be a degree of compromise.

The important considerations all teachers must bear in mind are:—

1. Is there a local/distant site I know which will give my pupils *practical* experiences to enhance mapping skills?
2. When we visit the site chosen what can mapwork contribute to the pupils' greater knowledge and understanding?

Principles to Follow

Fieldwork is a golden, but all too rare, opportunity for children to see, touch, smell, hear and relate to real places and people. It is vital to derive maximum benefit from such opportunities. We would suggest that great care be taken if worksheets are to be used. A badly prepared worksheet will ruin a visit.

A group of eight year olds visited a Commercial Vehicle Museum and were issued with worksheets. They wandered around the museum and read the printed cards displayed in front of the vehicles. Their worksheets were immaculate but they saw, touched and experienced nothing of any consequence. The size, shape, colour and design of the superb vehicles were hardly noticed in the pursuit of detailed knowledge.

We would suggest that before embarking on a visit pupils should be asked what they expect to find there. Their expectations and predictions can be compared with their post-visit reflections. Discussion should deal with what they want to take with them and what techniques should be used for *investigating* the site.

Sketchpads, notebooks, cameras and tape recorders should all be available. Let the fieldwork be an experience and an opportunity for collecting data. The data collected will form the basis of subsequent work in the classroom. Questions of fact, opinion and judgement can be raised after the visit by reference to the evidence the pupils bring back with them.

A variety of maps can be used before, during and after a visit. Prior to departure the pupils can identify the location of the site, describe the area around it, select landmarks and features they will look for 'en route'. They should work out the time the journey will take (time/distance/scale) and if public transport is to be used they should calculate costs and study timetables along with maps.

Appropriate maps should be used on the visit. These may be commercial or drawn by the pupils on site (they will need tape measures/trundle wheels/compasses/clipboards/strong paper).

Details noted by sketching, note taking or photography (slides/prints/video) can be added to the maps back at school. The map will provide the two-dimensional record which will enhance the photos and sketches in helping children understand the whole site.

In and Around a Church

The decline in church attendance ought to make us aware that many pupils will never have visited a church and the majority will not have been in a church when a service is taking place. This is an important point to bear in mind. Fieldwork, whenever possible, should explore not only the physical nature of the site but also the human aspect. We cannot expect fieldwork to be confined to Sundays but we can approach the vicars/rectors/ministers/priests and ask them to talk to the children about how the church is used *now* as well as about its history. Any children or adults who can be enlisted to demonstrate aspects of worship will also be of value.

The best OS map to use is undoubtedly the 1:1250 or 1:2500 (depending on whether your chosen church is urban or rural). The map will usually indicate the denomination.

The Churchyard

If the church has a *lychgate* it should be clear from the map. Few of them are earlier than the 17th century. Many are recent restorations.'Lych' is the old word for dead body. The coffin was rested at the lychgate while the priest said part of the burial service.

The benches in the Lychgate were for the bearers. A portable stand was carried for the coffin. Children are fascinated to learn that in Medieval England through to the 18th century many people were not buried in coffins. The coffin was owned by the parish. The body was removed prior to burial. From 1678 to 1814 to increase the revenue from the tax on wool it was compulsory to bury the dead in a woollen shroud.

Older churchyards may have a number of interesting features. Look out for trees marked on the map. The pupils can identify the type — by photographing, rubbing, sketching and collecting fallen leaves/fruit/twigs — and then using the evidence back in school with reference books.

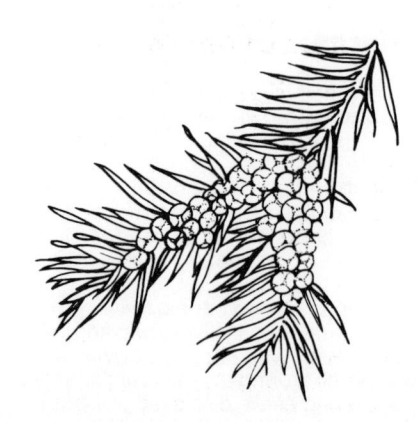

The Yew tree is still common in many churchyards. It lives longer than any other tree in Europe and many pre-date the churches they stand near. A few may be 1,500 years old and a number are certainly over a thousand years. Many local yews have exaggerated traditions attached to them and caution is always advisable. Edward I ordered yews to be planted near churches to act as a natural protection.

Crosses

Few churches have ancient crosses in the churchyard. If you are fortunate to have access to a churchyard which does, it is worthy of note. Crosses pre-dated the church in many cases. The cross was used for preaching from, while the church was under construction.

'Anglo-Saxon Cross'

Many crosses (or their bases) are to be found away from churches, at crossroads or on ancient routeways. They are marked on OS maps and pupils may wish to identify their location. Many crosses were destroyed during the Puritan supremacy and the crosses in position these days may be relatively modern. Some are memorials to those who died in the Great War but they often used the original cross base which is our evidence of past practices.

The Graveyard

The graveyard will fascinate pupils. In 'Discover Maps' pp. 4/5 we introduce some work on interpreting a headstone — this is first-hand historical evidence which children can read, record, rub with wax/heelbore or photograph. The writing of amusing epitaphs should not be regarded as bad taste. There are many examples of very humorous epitaphs in churchyards, some at the request of the deceased, others by relatives.

> *Epitaph on a pessimist*
> by Thomas Hardy
>
> *I'm Smith of Stoke, aged sixty-odd*
> *I've lived without a dame*
> *From youth-time on: and would to God*
> *My dad had done the same*

In overgrown churchyards you can peel vegetation from a gravestone. Take the vegetation back to school, pour quick setting plaster of paris on to it and you will have a cast of the original stone. Few headstones are earlier than the 17th century.

Churchyards have not always been treated with the respect that is now expected. Fairs were held in the churchyard, dancing and game playing also went on. Ale, brewed in the church, was served in the churchyard.

Some churchyards pre-date the church. They were pagan burial grounds which were adopted by the Christian community. In older churchyards the earliest graves are on the south side of the church. People did not want the shadow of the church to fall over their graves. The South side is also higher in many old churchyards. Bodies were buried one on top of the other thus raising the ground level over time.

Graves are normally aligned on an east-west axis. (Small scale mapping with compasses will show this, the pupils can discover this for themselves without being told). The origins of this pattern are to be found in the belief in bodily resurrection. Christians believed (and some still do) that at the 'second coming' Christ would come from the east. They were buried with their heads in the west so they could rise and be facing in the right direction. This custom is continued in many churchyards. Check whether headstones are at the western end of the grave.

Recent changes in churchyards (landscaping, building, even road widening) have resulted in many gravestones being moved. Some are laid side by side to form paths. It is important to assess if the graves you can see are as originally laid out or whether they have been moved.

There are many regional variations in the materials used for gravestones. Stone is usual but wood, iron, slate and other materials may be common in specific locations, and imported marble can be found in many graveyards.

Observing the Church

Observation is possible before you arrive. Let the pupils forecast whether the church has a spire/tower or neither. They will soon realise that the 1:1250/1:2500 does not provide the information. They will need to work through a variety of OS maps until they find the scale which offers the information they require. It is important that pupils are faced with these problems. In searching for the right map they are internalising the concept of different scales and different information.

Details of spires and towers can be found on OS scales of 1:25,000 and 1:50,000.

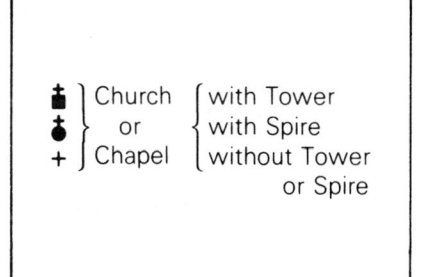

```
 ✠ ⎫ Church  ⎧ with Tower
 ♦ ⎬   or    ⎨ with Spire
 + ⎭ Chapel  ⎩ without Tower
                      or Spire
```

Children can map the external walls of the church. This is a much more interesting activity if the church has buttresses. Begin by standing back and trying to sketch the ground plan very roughly. Accurate measurement can then be carried out and the information used to produce a map which the child can 'picture'.

The children may well work out for themselves that buttresses support the church walls. As a very general rule the thinner the wall, the greater the buttress. Internal observation will show that buttresses are usually in line with the roof trusses.

Saxon (7th-11th centuries)

Decorated (14th century)

The size of windows varies with date. Pupils observations will identify that Saxon, Norman and Early English windows are smaller than windows constructed after the 13th Century. When asked why, they will often suggest that glass had not been invented. Glass, of course, was well known in medieval times, the inhibitor to use was cost. Many windows had other materials in them (parchment, oiled linen etc.) to keep out the wind and rain. Many such windows are splayed on the inside to allow more light into the body of the church. Improvements in building techniques and a reduction in the price of glass resulted in a growth in window sizes from the 13th to the 16th centuries.

'Discover Maps' p. 5 provides three window styles. The two shown here complete the range found in most older churches.

As with any visit to a historical site the teacher must be wary of what is original and what is a later 'replacement'. Our old industrial towns have superb classical buildings — but they were not built by Romans or Greeks! Similarly much church building of the nineteenth (and less so the twentieth) century looked backwards for its models and styles. Check the local church history before identifying 'original Saxon doors'.

Broad sketch mapping can take place inside a church. Observation will show pupils that most churches are divided into distinct areas.

The earliest, simplest plan was a simple *Nave* (body of the church) and sanctuary (at the eastern end of the church where the priest celebrated mass). Many churches developed into a cruciform plan. This overall plan can be seen on the 1:1250/1:2500 OS maps and can be labelled later following oral questioning during the visit and the later use of reference books back in school. The addition of a vestry, aisles and chantries may well have transformed the cruciform into a rectangle. Examination of the walls will often provide clues to the development pattern.

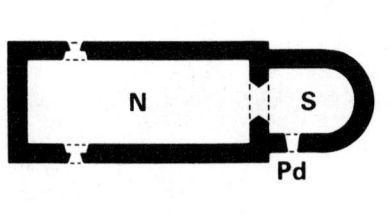

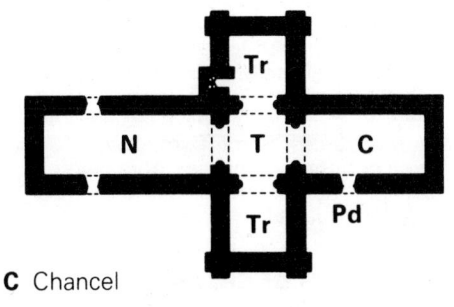

N Nave **S** Sanctuary **C** Chancel
T Tower **Tr** Transept **Pd** Priest's door

Exploring a Farm

Many pupils have a somewhat bizarre impression of farms and farmers. Harvest posters of farmers scattering seed by hand are part of the development of a picture of farming as an idyllic occupation frozen in time. We need to be clear with pupils that farming is an industry. It is increasingly specialised and mechanised. As with all industries farming ought to make maximum use of its resources — in farming terms this will include land, buildings, staff and machinery.

Changes in Farming

We need to recognise that farming is in another period of change. Food mountains, intervention prices and falling land values have all contributed to a period of upheaval. This can be an important focus for our work on a farm visit: *continuity and change*.

The farm featured in 'Discover Maps' p. 18 is a real farm which has been subject to these pressures for change. The range of interests shown on the map reflect the shift towards leisure activities which many farmers have been encouraged to make. The caravans indicate tourism, the horses an increased interest in riding by those who may live in towns but have leisure time and resources. Some farms have switched their emphases from dairy cattle to beef or sheep since milk quotas were introduced.

Indicators of Change

The pupils can investigate evidence of change. This may be obvious (e.g. a milking parlour on a sheep farm) or it may be more subtle (freshly planted woodland). The use of 1:2500/1:10,000 maps will help in this investigation. New woodland will not appear on the map and will need to be marked. A new toilet block to serve caravans will not be shown on the range of farm buildings. Oral interviews with the farmer will elicit information about changes of use.

The farm shown in 'Discover Maps' is a mixed farm but it grows no crops except grass to feed the sheep/cattle/horses in winter. Pupils need to know that the notion of a farm which keeps pigs, cows, sheep, horses, hens and goats and which grows potatoes, wheat, sugar beet, cabbage and peas is a myth.

The principles used in the pupils' book can be transferred to your own fieldwork whether you visit a mixed farm or a farm which is highly specialised in growing arable crops, fruit or vegetables.

Preparation for the Visit

Good practice behoves us to start from where the children are. There is no reason to suppose that the vast majority of pupils will ever have visited a farm.

It is useful to begin by *brainstorming*. The children simply list what they expect to find at the farm. This will help the teacher to identify the starting point of the work. A repeat exercise can be carried out at the end of the topic and the responses will contribute towards the evaluation.

On the basis of the brainstorming supportive preparatory work can be designed. A variety of OS maps on which the farm is shown can be introduced. This is tangible evidence which will focus pupil thinking. Questions can be raised and discussed — how many fields are there? What will we find in them? How many people work and live there? Are they men/women/children? What are the buildings used for? What machinery will we find? Whenever possible the pupils should generate these questions but often they will need strong teacher guidance.

What ought to emerge is the group's perception of what it does not know and the subsequent identification of a schedule for investigation. 'What do we want to find out? What will we look for? What is the best way to find out?' Thus if some pupils want to know how a woman on the farm spends her day, they may decide to compile a schedule of questions and take along a tape recorder. The posing, drafting, asking and recording of questions are important skills and it is important not to spoon-feed pupils in these activities.

Observation and Recording

Use the 1:2500 maps to examine the buildings and immediate area of the farm and record the results in sketches and notes. Observation of building and field uses will require the development on site of an appropriate key. Here the pupils will be practising specific mapping skills in a real-life situation when the activity can be seen to have a purpose. If you want the group to develop colour keys then you will need to have coloured pencils/felt tips available on site (alternatively you can use a shorthand of abbreviations). The pupils could design their own symbols as an alternative to colours. The essential point to remember is to draw the key first so that pupils can then re-interpret the data they collect.

Field boundaries

These are shown on OS maps up to the 1:25,000 scale. What is not shown is whether they are hedges, wooden fences, open border, post and wire fences etc.

The starting point is to check whether the field boundaries shown on the map correspond with current boundaries. If they do not, the children should note the changes. Once mapped the boundaries can be identified by materials used. This opens up the question of continuity and the related issue of conservation. Encourage the children to look for patterns; are fields becoming larger or smaller? Is there a reason for the changes? Does the removal of a hedge have an impact on the countryside? These issues can be explored from different points of view.

How do the changes affect the visual appearance of the rural area? Does it affect the quality of the soil? Is wildlife affected by the disappearance of hedgerows and if so how?

Changes in the rural economy mean that simple answers no longer apply. In the past the loss of hedgerows could have been a question of efficiency/cost. Now, if the area is to be developed for leisure and tourism, the visual (aesthetic) aspect of the area needs to be considered. Interviews with different groups will inform pupil attitudes.

Urban Fieldwork

COULD YOU TELL ME WHAT YOU ARE DOING IN THIS AREA?

All pupils should have opportunities to explore and investigate rural and urban locations. Urban fieldwork will be improved by the appropriate use of 1:1250/1:10;000 maps.

One starting point for urban fieldwork is to begin with an exploration of your immediate environment, be it rural or urban. This will provide a data-base and fieldwork experience. You will be able to compare the urban setting you visit with your own location.

Choose a location which is manageable and safe and select a series of focuses on which you will concentrate.

Street Furniture

A 1:1250 map is ideal for marking street furniture. The location of street lamps, manhole covers, grids, post and telephone boxes etc. can be measured and noted. Rubbings, sketches, notes and photographs can be taken. This will be displayed to good effect around a map extract. This provides a visual translation of 2-D to 3-D.

Using Photographs

The camera and video camera can contribute significantly to an evaluation of the studied environment. Pupils should be encouraged to study locations from the perspective of quality and with a view to making statements about how it might be improved. If pavements and/or roads are uneven, pitted or cracked it can be recorded on film. Is there a great quantity of litter or dog dirt every metre? Is street furniture ideally placed for those who need to use it?

Changes and improvements which the class suggest can be demonstrated with drawings, written statements and maps appropriately marked.

Oral Evidence

Oral work should centre on the interviewing of a number of people who live, work or shop in the vicinity. The questions should be short and designed to elicit information which is easy to handle. Longer interviews should be taped or video recorded and used to develop a theme further.

Buildings

This area of enquiry ought to include materials and functions as well as styles and categories.

Once again this is best achieved in a small scale but detailed investigation using a 1:1250 map. However, if a picture of a wider area is required different groups can do 'sample' work in different sectors of a 1:10,000 extract. Remember to look at roofs, chimneys, walls, windows, doors, garden features for style and materials. Look too for evidence of change. This is most obvious when only one house in an area appears to be built of different materials. This was common on Council estates when the right to buy was established. Many buyers felt the need to have their home distinguished from those around. Porches and new windows were popular but some opted to replace brick with stone on some walls.

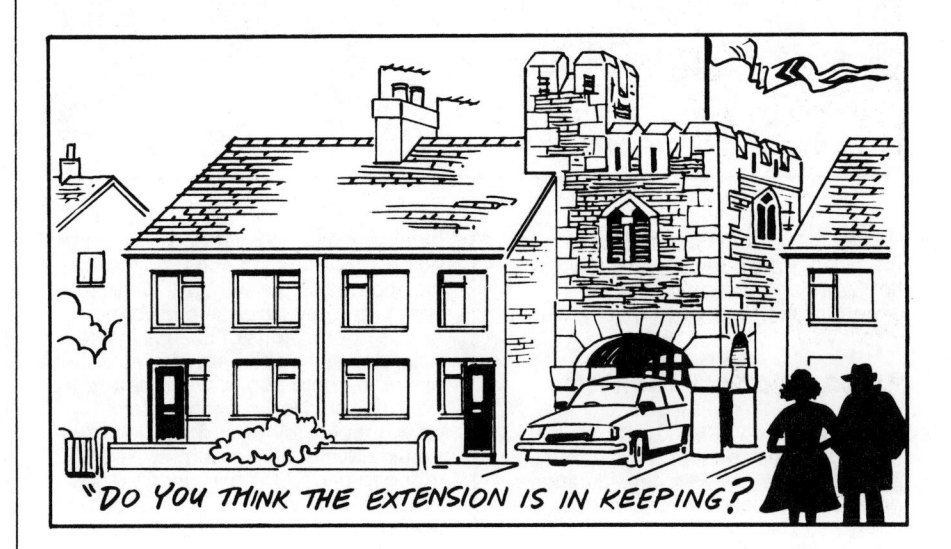

"DO YOU THINK THE EXTENSION IS IN KEEPING?"

The functions of the buildings will need to be categorised in such a way as to be meaningful to the pupils. Younger children may find a two-way classification sufficient —
shops or houses — whereas older pupils will use a key on the map and may classify by shops, offices, banks, schools, factories, warehouses, entertainment, public houses, places of worship, etc. The 1:1250 will facilitate this in a street, the 1:10,000 will be appropriate for the pattern in an area. A colour key will soon identify areas of land usage —

Industrial	Service	Housing	Recreation etc.

Taking a Census

Shopping, traffic and housing censuses can all be carried out in an identified urban location and the resulting data compared with data from your own school's environment.

The concept of *similarity and difference* should always be at the forefront of the teacher's mind when engaging in fieldwork.

SHOPPING CENSUS					
Newsagents	Baker	Butcher	DIY	P.O.	

√ = 1 person   √√√√√ = 5

Investigating a Castle

FANCY BUILDING A CASTLE SO CLOSE TO THE BUS STATION!

'Master Maps' examines a castle on pp. 6/7. Castles are popular with schools for fieldwork and the quality of the experience is improved if maps are used effectively.

Preparation for the Visit

Prior to a visit a 1:50,000 or 1:25,000 OS map should be consulted and discussed by the group. The key consideration here is the location of the castle.

Is it built on high land?
How can we tell from the map?
If it is on high land why would the builders have chosen such a site?
Is it built near a river, lake or the sea?

Once again we need to know what possible potential advantages such a location would offer to the builders. The 1:25,000 will show the castle shape more clearly and its immediate local features. The 1:50,000 will provide evidence of any other castles in the area and will therefore raise questions about the reasons why series of castles were sometimes built.

The 1:10,000 OS map should be used next. It will show the features of the castle much more clearly and it will provide evidence of whether the castle was attached to walls which ran around the local settlements. This is a common feature in many castles (Caernarfon is one such) and at its simplest level this should elicit from the group that the castle provided protection for the town's inhabitants and that danger probably threatened from outside.

The 1:1250/1:2500 OS maps can be used next but it is often better to obtain plans of the castle from the appropriate authorities.

The Visit

Discussion during the visit should centre on the purposes the castle served and the people who lived in it. Many pupils are astonished to learn that not every castle was filled to overflowing with powerful barons, heavily armoured knights and women in wimples who spent most of the day looking out of the window while they completed their massive embroidery. Artists impressions of castles in use are helpful to many children. Many teachers prefer to show pupils these before the visit. Others like to examine an open-topped tower and ask whether it would always have been so. The wooden parts of most older castles have disappeared and if not replaced present a misleading image to the children.

The Castle Plan will help with a discussion of design. Are the towers round, square or hexagonal? Which is the best design from a defensive point of view?

Such questions can lead to construction work back in the classroom. Small towers can be subjected to bombardment and the effects recorded.

The plan may also offer clues to the past usage of parts of the castle. Often sections may be named — the 'Well Tower' should not be too hard to interpret.

Some castles can arrange for children to use specially equipped rooms with artefacts. Others have costumes which the pupils wear in order to act out everyday events from the past. Even without such props children's imaginations can be fired by encouraging them to use part of the castle (the dungeon goes down well) for role-play. This can make the visit come alive for many young people.

The group should record the building materials used, the orientation of spiral stairways, they should take rubbings where allowed and photographs when appropriate.

It is also useful to examine changes made to the castle. Many castles now have entrances which are relatively recent. The castle when built may well have had a drawbridge leading to an artificial embankment. Children should look for such alterations.

One way of tackling this issue is to give the children roles —

'if you were designing the defences of this castle . . .'
'if you wanted to attack this castle where do you think its weakest point would be?'

Following the route of potential attackers will highlight defensive features. Sharp 90° turns are built into many internal castle routeways. Narrow arrow slits are located before and after the portcullis. At each step pupils will identify defensive features and these can then be marked on the plan for follow-up work back at school. Castles are superb places for children as long as they are free to think, imagine and discuss. A badly constructed worksheet is capable of destroying the 'feel' of the castle. We would advise caution in the use of 'closed' question worksheets on castle visits.

While on the castle walls it is a golden opportunity to look down at the area around with the appropriate section of a 1:10,000 OS map. The street patterns, buildings, waterways and open spaces will all be seen. It is the nearest thing to an aerial photograph. Maps take on a new meaning for many children after such an experience.

The castle towers had sloping wooden roofs.

Using Old Maps

Maps Ancient and Modern

The use of maps to investigate the past is growing in many shcools. The objective is to identify historical change, in order to do so the pupil needs to use a variety of mapping skills.

'Discover Maps' and 'Master Maps' devote space to the theme of old and new maps.

CONCEPT OF CHANGE: DEVELOPED IN	
'Discover Maps' pp. 12/13 pp. 14/15	'Master Maps' pp. 2/3 pp. 14/15 pp. 20/21

It is worth obtaining prints of older maps from Roman times and from the later Middle Ages. The uses of colour, decoration, symbols etc. can all be discussed. More recent mapping invites closer analysis.

Saxton's maps from the 16th Century are available for many counties (N.B. they refer to the former British County System and are not necessarily of your current county. Check which county your school was in prior to 1974 before attempting to obtain a map such as Saxton's. This advice holds good for all pre '74 mapping. The point is one to be explored with the children — many of whom will be perplexed that a town can move from one county to another. This opens up a debate on borders and why and how they are changed.

In some parts of the country this may be a 'live' local issue. For example, should Salop be called Shropshire? Can someone from Westmorland ever accept being known as a Cumbrian? What has been done with Caernarfonshire, Rutland etc.?

When examining older maps there is real investigative work to be done in exploring some of the principles pupils are now expected to follow. Why do old maps have boats, fish and even people on them? Why are buildings drawn on flat rather than as plan view? Why are mountains also drawn rather than use contours?

Place Names

Place name analysis can be exciting detective work, especially if the school has reference books which chart the development and change of place names over the years. This can be allied with an analysis of the meanings of place names. Remember however that the origin of a place name is no guarantee that the settlement had its origin in a certain period. A Saxon place name (e.g. — ton) simply tells us that there was a settlement there in Saxon times. It could however have simply been a change of name for a pre-Saxon British settlement, the name of which is now lost to us.

Decoding old scripts is a part of reading historical maps. It is also worthwhile to take old names and compare them with European locations. The Saxon map on p. 2 of 'Master Maps' refers to 'Leverpoole haven' — an examination of North European maps will throw up countless ports which include 'haven', or a corruption of it, in their names.

Comparisons between sixteenth century and modern maps can be enhanced by comparing intervening maps as well. It is then sometimes possible to identify the approximate dates when changes occurred.

RECORD OF CHANGE

1890 Temperance Hall	1932 Cinema	1989 Disco

Local Maps

The same is true of local maps. A series of maps observed in their chronological order will allow pupil analysis of change. The changes wrought in Birmingham within a hundred years ('Discover Maps' p. 12/13) are major and the similarities are few. The same is not the case in the maps on 'Master Maps' p. 20/21 where the street pattern remains essentially the same but the land use changes dramatically.

The impact of the maps and their contributions to pupil learning will be greatly increased if they are accompanied by photographs/drawings/paintings of the period when the map was drawn. Those within living memory would be further enhanced by interviewing old people who might refer to the earlier maps and bring them alive by describing the place, its people and well remembered events. In this way the combination of map, pictorial and oral evidence provides a well rounded picture of the past.

Theme Maps

Theme maps are available, often free, from a wide variety of sources. Estate Agents, Tourist Boards, Holiday Companies, Motoring Organisations etc. all produce their own maps for those who may wish to use their services. The key idea behind a 'theme' map is that it is not comprehensive — it *selects* the information relevant to the readers' interests and it stresses such information and often excludes other detail.

A guide to 'places to eat' in a city centre will not provide benchmarks or local government boundaries. If it refers to Post Offices, railway stations or public buildings it will do so solely in order to provide landmarks for those who wish to find a place to eat.

The theme maps of 'Knowsley Safari Park' ('Discover Maps' pp. 20/21) and of Ealing Broadway Shopping Centre ('Master Maps' pp. 12/13) are examples of the type. They contribute to the pupil's understanding of the value and function of maps. In the shopping centre the map is a tool to assist our shopping. We know where to go to find specific items. We can therefore use our time more effectively.

The Safari Park map ignores scale and contour. The lion is not really larger than the road but it helps us to see that the 'area' is where lions are found.

Local theme maps, produced for particular purposes are an ideal introduction to mapwork for many children. They are clearly utilitarian and pupils can therefore recognise relevance and purpose. All their information appears relevant and there is little 'filtering' required of a kind which will be needed with most other maps. Some basic applications of maps can therefore be introduced through theme maps, but it is important to recognise their limitations as well as their strengths and pupils whose diet is confined to such maps will never be truly literate in maps.

Answers to the Worksheets

Answers are provided for those worksheets where the right answers are not immediately obvious.

Page

13. View point 7
1. a) Male Staff Toilet
   b) Girls' Toilet 2
   c) Female Staff Toilet
2. a) Dining Room
   b) Male Staff Toilet
   c) Library
3. a) West
   b) North
   c) South
4. a) North
   b) East
   c) West
   d) South
5. Open Ended

16. Symbols 2
1.

Picture	Symbol	Description
A	3	Campsite
B	2	Golf course
C	6	Church with spire
D	4	Viewpoint
E	1	Picnic Site
F	5	Skiing

2. Child should draw pictures of
   a) Telephone box   c) A school
   b) Wildlife park   d) A bus station

3. a) P   b) 🏕
   c) ⬬   d) 〰

17. Symbols 3
1. A = ↑, N = ◯, E = 𝟪,
   Z = ←, L = ✈
2. ⌽ = C, ? = G, ✈ = L,
   ◯ = N, △ = Y
3. Open ended.
4. Tomorrow is a school holiday.
5.
6. Open ended.
7.

19. Symbols 5: Teacher Assessment

21. Direction 1
1.

Left	Centre	Right
Kennels	Pigs	Cows
Hens	Farmhouse	Barn
Silo	Kennels	Pigs
Orchard	Machinery	Lambs
Stables	Garden	Pond
Goats	Hens	Farmhouse

2.

	Left	Right
A	Stables	Garden
A	Hens	Farmhouse
A	Kennels	Pigs
A	Machinery	Lambs
B	Garden	Pond
B	Farmhouse	Barn
B	Pigs	Cows
B	Lambs	
C	Goats	Stables
C	Hens	Stables
C	Farmhouse	Garden
C	Barn	Pond
D	Silo	Goats
D	Kennels	Hens
D	Pigs	Farmhouse
D	Cows	Barn

22. Direction 2
1.⎫ The colours selected for the
2.⎭ key should match the map.

3. a) Birds
   b) Fountain
   c) Giraffes
4. a) Elephants
   b) Picnic Area
   c) Giraffes
5. a) Kangaroos
   b) Fountain
   c) Rhinoceros
6. a) Monkeys
   b) Toilets
   c) Picnic Area

23. Direction 3
1.

Pet	Start	Directions
Cat	A	E,N,E,S,E,N
Rabbit	A	E,N,E,S,E,S,E,N,E,S
Bird	A	E,N,E,S,E,S,E,N,E,S
Fish	A	E,N,E,S,E,S,E,S,W
Mouse	B	S,E,N,E,S,W,S
Snake	B	S,E,S,W,N,W,S
Tortoise	B	S,W,S

2.

Pet	Directions to the till
Puppy	N,E,N,E,S,E,S,E
Cat	S,W,S,E,S,E
Rabbit	N,W,S,W,N,W,S,E,S,E
Bird	N,W,S,W,N,W,S,E,S,E
Fish	E,N,W,N,W,S,E
Mouse	N,E,S,E
Snake	N,E,S,E,N,E,S,E
Tortoise	N,E,S,E,N,E,S,E

24. Direction 4
1. a) North East is halfway between N and E.
   b) South East is halfway between S and E.
   c) South West is halfway between S and W.
2. a) NW b) NE c) SE d) SW e) W f) E.

3.

Start	Stop	Direction
Slide	Boating	NE
Ice cream	Roundabout	W
Riding	Boating	SW
Ice cream	Sand	SW
Climbing frame	Golf	N
Golf	Ice cream	SW
Sand	Ice cream	NE
Roundabout	Boating	E
Sand	Boating	NW

25. Direction 5

		Bearing in °	Compass Direction
Lighthouse	🗼	090°	E
Golf	⚑	135°	SE
Telephone	☎	180°	S
Castle	Castle	225°	SW
Bus station	⬢	270°	W
Town Hall	T.H.	315°	NW
Church with tower	✚	360°	N
Post Office	P	045°	NE

Page

27. Scale 1

2.

	CASTLE A		CASTLE B	
	Height	Width	Height	Width
Door	2cm	2cm	4cm	4cm
Window	2cm	1cm	4cm	2cm
Tower	6cm	3cm	12cm	6cm

28. Scale 2

4.

	A	B
Height of clown	12cm	24cm
Length of foot	2½cm	5cm
Height of hat	1cm	2cm
Width of shoulders	3cm	6cm

31. Scale 5

Depending on the age and manual dexterity of the pupils teacher, discretion should allow a degree of latitude.
Approximate to 1m.

1.

Person	Journey	Distance
Warren	Maths table	9m
Shanaz	Science table	5m
Ruth	Teacher's desk	4m
Ben	Teacher's desk	3m
Sima	Door	9m
Feroz	Bookshelves	10m
Tina	Door	3m
Jo	Window	7m

2. Children should compare
3. plans.

33. Routes 1

1.

Room Symbol	Using a ruler		In real life	
	Width	Length	Width	Length
CL. 1	3cm	4cm	6m	8m
♪	4cm	7cm	8m	14m
(broom)	1cm	1½cm	2m	3m
(pan)	1½cm	3cm	3m	6m
(girl)	1½cm	2cm	3m	4m

2. Children should compare plans.
3a) Children should discuss and compare estimates.

b)

Route	Estimate	String Measurement
Red	Openended	23m
Blue	"	17m
Green	"	32m
Orange	"	22m
Purple	"	23m
Yellow	"	46m

34. Routes 2

1.

	Using a Ruler	Real Life
Main St.	16cm	160m
Cross St.	16cm	160m
Park Rd.	10cm	100m
Back Lane	10cm	100m
Moon Cres.	4cm	40m
Bent Row	2cm	20m

2a) Open ended

c)

Colour	From	To	Distance
Red	PS	N	100m
Blue	BG	Sch	110m
Yellow	10 Main St.	12 Cross St.	160m
Green	12 Back Lane	B	95m
Orange	⊕	LC	55m
Purple	7 Moon Cres	PO	115m
Pink	F	(duck)	210m

37. Grid References 1

1.

Grid Ref.	Picture	Description
A2		Spaceship
C5		Alien
G4		Jellyteens
D4		Munch machine
B4		Spaceship

2.

Contact	Grid References
Spaceships	A2, B4, F1, F5
Aliens	C2, C5, F3, G7
Munch machines	A5, D4, D7
Jellyteens	A7, D1, E6, G4

3. Check rockets in grid squares C3, D5, G3, B7, D2, A1, E4, F2
4. D3, F6

40. Grid References 4

1a)

Grid Ref.	Description
18, 40	Rat
19, 42	Cauldron
20, 46	Castle
16, 44	Witch's cat
14, 45	Poison
15, 46	Witch

b)

Grid Ref.	Description
17, 46	Ghost with big feet
15, 42	Lady with no head
18, 43	Spells book
18, 45	Broomstick
19, 44	House
17, 41	Frogs

41. Grid References 5

The map should be similar to 1-10.

11. Cross check legend with map

Page

43. Location 1

1.

Area	Letter
Art & Craft	B
Computers	D
Child's place	F
Stock room	G
Teacher's desk	E
Maths cupboard	C
Reading corner	A

2.

Location	Activity
B	Paint a picture
A	Choose a book
D	Use a computer
G	Store spare paper
C	Get a pair of scales
B	Wash a paintbrush

44. Location 2

1.

Location	Activity
E	Catch fish
F	Look at peacocks
B	Build a sandcastle
D	Playing rolling downhill on the grass
C	Eat a picnic beside the pond
A	Play football
G	Bandage a cut leg

2.

Land Surface	Location
Flat	A, B, E, F
Sloping	C, G
Steep	D

3 and 4 Open ended

48. Height 2

3.

A	1
B	3
C	0
D	4
E	2

4. D, B, E, A, C

49. Height 3

Number 2 is the side view

Collins Educational
OS Resource Book

Pupil Checklist

NAME ....

CLASS ....

X performed competently

STAGE 1

Match picture/plan	
Draw plans of everyday objects	
Draw plan of table top	
Draw plan of classroom from observation	
Draw classroom routes on plan	
Compare oblique/side/plan view	
Read and interpret a school plan	
Follow a journey to school on OS 1250/2500	
Draw simple mental map	
Use colour key	
Use symbol key	
Make own symbols	
Recognise basic OS symbols	
Give directions using N. S. E. W.	
Estimate lengths	
Use arbitrary measurements e.g. paces	
Record measurements in chart form	
Use 2 fig. grid ref. (letter/number)	
Depict height in drawings	
Model making to different heights	
Observe and discuss heights of local landmarks	
Familiar with aerial photographs	

STAGE 2

Draw classroom plan using arbitrary measurements	
Use plan of school to locate points on a route	
Draw routes on a local map	
Align a map with features in the locality	
Describe a location on OS 1:1250/1:2500	
Draw plan of house using symbols	
Make an appropriate symbol key	
Recognise OS symbols	
Cross reference OS symbols map/key	
Use a compass to find North	
Give accurate directions	
Use ½ (1:2) scale	
Use ¼ (1:4) scale	
Reduce and enlarge to scale	
Use string to measure routes to scale	
Use number/number grid references	
Plot 2 figure grid references	
Depict height differences with colour	
Make a colour relief key	
Recognise colour relief on map	
Use aerial photographs of small local area (familiar location)	

STAGE 3

Draw a plan of classroom to scale	
Draw a plan of room at home to scale	
Draw a plan of school using a key	
Recognise most OS symbols	
Follow route using 8 point compass	
Design orienteering course	
Give map directions	
Able to choose appropriate scale	
Estimate accurately	
Record accurately	
Recognise maps for different purposes	
Plot routes on maps	
Recognise official and unofficial routes	
Give coordinates using Easting/Northing	
Use 4 figure grid reference	
Describe the buildings in a grid square	
From a written description identify a location on OS 1:25,000	
Recognise contour lines where layer colouring meets	
Use aerial photos for land use	

STAGE 4

Draw a map of the locality	
Draw plans to scale	
Recognise networks	
Describe an area using key and relief features	a) local / b) national / a) Urban / b) Rural
Give written description of a grid sq. 1:25,000	
Use circular protractor	
Follow and give bearing instructions	
Describe a journey using locational language of	a) local environment / b) alternative environment
Choose appropriate scale in map making	
Use linear scale with ease	
Use a variety of scales	
Use 6 fig. grid references	
Make accurate comparisons between Aerial photo and OS map	a) 1:25,000 / b) 1:50,000
Read contour lines to describe relief	
Draw contour lines to depict relief	

© Collins Educational: Harrisons/OS Resource Book ▶ You may photocopy this page for use in the classroom ◀ 63

Acknowledgements
Linda Edmondson
Derek Earnshaw
Jim Page
Eddie Ketley
Malcolm Watson

Important Notice
Purchase of this book allows permission to photocopy the following pages for classroom use:
Pages 7–13, 15–19, 21–25, 27–31, 33–35, 37–41, 43–45, 47–49, 51–52, 63.

Design by Barrie Richardson

Illustration by Brick, Stephen Gaffney, Val Saunders, Tim Smith and Shirley Wheeler.

© 1989 Holmes McDougall/Ordnance Survey
© 1989 Text: Patricia and Steve Harrison

All rights reserved. No part of this publication may be reproduced, stored in a retrieval system or transmitted in any form or by any means whether electronic, mechanical, photocopying, recording or otherwise, or translated into another language without the permission of the publishers and copyright holders, except where noted otherwise.

Ordnance Survey Maps reproduced with the permission of The Controller, Her Majesty's Stationery Office. Crown copyright reserved. Copyright 1989.

First published 1989 by Holmes McDougall Ltd.
Published in 1991 by
CollinsEducational
An imprint of HarperCollins*Publishers*
77–85 Fulham Palace Road
Hammersmith
London W6 8JB

Reprinted 1992

ISBN 0 00 316 138 2

Printed in Great Britain by Antony Rowe Ltd, Chippenham, Wiltshire